CW00590441

Words and cover art by Mitchell Burke,
Cover design by wilder (@wilderpoetry)

The Corner of The Room © by Mitchell Burke,
all rights reserved, no section or part of this book may be
reproduced or replicated without written permission
from the author.

Follow @m.nihilist on Instagram for new poems daily.

ISBN: 978-1975707934

Foreward

I've been writing poetry for years now. The moment I began can't be pinpointed to a specific time but ever since, I've been wondering why I even blessed myself with this curse. I don't consider myself as a writer necessarily. I know you can get technical with it and look up the definition and relate me to this picture painted by words, but in reality, I'm just a human trying to get by in the easiest way possible. It seems to contradict itself, I just noticed the oxymorons being thrown at my face when putting this book together. I was copy and pasting old pieces into the manuscript and reading them in a sad memoriam, an antonym to reverence even. Seeing the state I was put and put myself in really made me realize how a medication can really prolong the reason for taking it in the first place. It destroyed me, putting me back into the shoes I was in, shoes that barely fit or, fit too big. It's August 2nd, 2017, as I'm sitting on the trunk of my car writing this foreward. Swigging this night into my chest as the fog covers the moon just barely like a horny nightgown. I can see silhouettes of willow trees in the distance splitting the corn field in half. Coming to a sense of sudden realization that every word I have ever written has entirely split my mind in half, my emotions in half, my morals in half. Writing about drinking, about heartbreak, about suicide, sex, about seeing death, feeling death and watching people with nosey eyes and a contradicting cocksure. This "gift" as my mother calls it, didn't come wrapped but ended up wrapping me in this horny nightgown letting out the light that was held captive by the darkness prior to knowing I could write what I couldn't speak. The contents of this book have torn me apart, they've gnawed at my heartstrings, they've helped me and fed me the strength to continue. This is not for money, for fame, this is showing the world that even the damaged can stare forward, this is a display that shows that even words can save lives and in this case, my own. I want this dying art to come back to life, I want the kids to read before bed and feel with their eyes again, I want the hurting to hurt less with the medication of shared suffering. This isn't meant to hold your vision for a quick moment, this is meant to tattoo my situations, my heartbreak, and my struggles in your mind forever. A mixture of brevity and lengthiness will present itself before your eyes. This passion, this art is dying with the "callous and murderous" youth. This heart spilling, mind-numbing prose is on the deathbed of existence, bludgeoned by laziness and attentiveness to the irrelevant. So if you're reading this, you're the light in darkness, you're the saviour to an art that needs saving.

Welcome to my heart, welcome to my life, welcome to my mind, welcome to, "The Corner of the Room".

The Corner of the Room

For the believers,
the disbelievers
and everyone in between,
for Mom
for Dad
for Hannah,
I love you all.

Sea Sick

an intrepid image of consistency to living painlessly
floats aimlessly through an adjacent sea of
complacency that finds a way to drift further from
shore, worries of capsizing and baptizing
in this ocean of social chastising
leaves me coming back for more.
descending the sail paints
images of pale
skies clouding progression,
shadowing the sun's oppression
to shining through the cracks,
dreams reflect the water
of sailing to shore and
never coming back,
the table in cabin
covered with cigarettes butts
and empty bottles,
leaving stains of black
on the whispering floorboards
that sways with the current
that restores more
contentedness to being
lost at sea.

but, I wake up to reality sea sick.

Emancipation Intoxication

It's a race to the bottom of the bottle
between sanity and sober realization
to every impaired negation and how to
alleviate and mediate the dependancy I
place on finding new routes to the
end of the drink —
the hands of the bottle hold
dreaded burdens above my head,
bringing life to each breath of morrow,
the hands write hymns towards yearning
a long awaited wish for death,
sobriety weaves this addiction
of solitude through each thought of
a halted life, and pushes its back
as its heels leave crevices to follow,
a view of darkness to come,
with turning back placing another knot
down a throat with attempt to swallow,
as each run of whiskey drips down the
walls of my throat, the sinking ship within
my veins finds strength to stay afloat,
a wallowing whisper tickles at the anticipations
towards taking another sip,
the tendencies stutter
a bodily equilibrium captivating
and inching my sanity towards
a shot of sequel librium —

as vomit spews and consumes
the inhabited ground, a paroxysm
of unconsciousness feels
mentally sound,
blacked out with the following
morning full of acts to repent,
the momentary blackness
proves to be nothing but content,
recollection of priors
seem to fade with the desire of
sobriety and eliminating any hope
towards thoughtless propriety —
momentary happiness through
intoxication provides no mediation
between a sober fight for death
and a drunken one, the wish for
lifelessness is just subdued by
stumbling to bed and the inability
to steadily hold a gun to my head.

Fuse

the fuse towards self-destruction
has finally been lit,
it's a slow burn to the
moment to where I finally quit,
I've had everything I've
ever wanted, yet not needed.
I've sat listening to these
demons whispering
as I pleaded for them to stop,
I've made a name for
myself within this city,
one that drips across my
sanity and carves
paths for demons to tip toe
to the back of my mind
and surface whenever I seem to find
a situation of serenity,
or an instance robbing
a common identity,
numbness has conquered
inclination with help
from lacking reciprocation,
a scarred back easing into a bed
with dangling threads from a home knitted
form of stability, a bed that straps any form
of mobility, leaving a struggling being
beneath the shackles that confine
a mind that finds time to rewind to when

sleep was sheep counted and not a moment
where peace was surmounted by nihility,
where the only versatility comes within
which ways are easier to kill me,

each day awoken leaves the devilish
mutters unspoken,
aesthetics show nothing but a painted
demeanour that dredges only when
the edges of the bed tremor as the
pillows inhale every scream and plea,

mornings are mournings for
how much I died the day before
and how each night brings
awakening as nothing to ever adore,
paralyzed limbs, every day, find way
to slide off the mattress,
stand up feeling backless,
stare to my hands and see
shakes as the burden of
consciousness snakes its
way through aspirations
like rolling fog that weakens
the foundation for social relations,

step out the door to broken
pavement, and whistling trees
that shower leaves to the dampened
green, bringing the melody of
tires to wet gravel
crushing the goal to unravel
this falsified disposition

writing today's edition of
"why the fuck didn't I stay in bed"

the sun goes down with the booze
so smooth to my throat keeping this body
staying afloat for one more night,
drink again and
feel this swaying ocean of liquor
rip an anesthetic of amnesia
knowing I can never please her,

the time has finally come where
I dip my hands into the keyboard
and plea for a release as my
eyes hide under a blanket
of stained glass masking
a pained past;
toxins flow slowly to my brain
through the uneasy flow of
each vain, poisoning every figment
of liver, as I vomit up every promise
I failed to deliver.

Yesterday

it seems like just yesterday we
were twisting our bodies beneath
the symphony of the moonlight,
singing songs of everlasting
love with no sight of ending,
from the beginning I knew
there would be some halt
of companionship as a result
of a stagnant feeling that I was enough
for how perfect you are,
there's nothing left of my pride
only the need to subside
from every burden I cause,
every day I woke up and
rolled over to you
laying there with serenity
thoughts collapses to emotion
knowing you thought you
were losing me, when
the state of my health
screamed out to me
assuring me I was losing myself,
so an awaited day finally came
where I let you go only to know
that you couldn't live without me,
seeing your distress left me
more of a mess than what I was before,
the only hope left within was the feeling
that you'd finally cope with me leaving

and find another soul that wouldn't
constantly leave a hole
in your heart every time my insecurities
would birth,
mistake after mistake fuelled by
instances I knew I couldn't take,
as you left after I did,
I knew I couldn't rid
myself from the way I felt
but the reassurance that
you'd be looked at one day
by eyes that held no despise for
their self, helped me,
I now bask in order to
mediate my conscience
to be sane,
accompanied by pills
that rip the morals
from my brain,
cigarette packs are emptying faster than
the bottle, pills to make me happy I swallow
and pills that numb, pull me closer to the edge
as I use my thumb to pop the lid, to push my
consumption of poison to dredge every sense of life
from this already lifeless body,
step out of your once loved mindset towards
my mistaken excuse for a being
and open your expectations to those that
exceed what you once held for me,
there's a room full of people right for you;
quit pounding on the door,
I'm not on the other side.

Nocturnus (Content) Pt. I

it's quiet and I hear nothing but the snowflakes
hit the fabric on my shoulder
I hear nothing but the paper
burn as my inhale imitates the gust of
wind that guides the cold to shutter skin —
street lights sit above the lit, white-flowered flakes
as they dance to the ground as a group
that whisper soliloquies to the crimson
lobes that hear nothing but the snowflakes
hit the fabric on my shoulder,
a hazy fog covers the air before my face
as it sways from nostril to upper lip —
a sight down to an illuminating ash,
blinking to meet a lid to whited lash —
the paper burns,
the smokey sky is content
with silence and nothing more
then a look to the fields.

Fumus (Discontent) Pt. II

it's 12 degrees outside
excluding the breeze, I hide
behind the rising smoke
of the cigarette just lit,
my fingers are falling off,
nails ripping to the marrow
a bodily stutter impairing speech,
a seizure and a grab to the fleeced pocket
leaves only the other hand to freeze,
such a sacrifice to something
the little boy I was said I didn't need,
I kick around snow
as my leather boots wear a
coat of white as I shiver
and inspire, throwing a black
coat over my lungs
"hey, do you have a lighter?"
"yeah"
the ash sails down
and kisses the filter and a flick
collides the ember to exhale its final breath
to the frozen floor,
I step inside and
suddenly, I'm cold again.

<u>He</u>

he goes searching for love in the wrong ways
guided in directions by bedsheets and lost
by indulgence in the temporary
decadence and narcissism
—

a mapless journey lead in the retrospected
direction of peer fulfilled gratification,
met already past the point of no return
by a social gathering of perceptions
and conceptions towards a tangible
reason
—

the smell of sweat,
consecutive exhales and inhales
pinpoint reminders after the fact,
held tight by only bedsheets,
watching her get dressed
pulling what she wore out
that night over a coiffure
of tangled penitence
as it rises above the
neck of her shirt
—

sitting amidst the marrow
of vision lies an exiting
woman, usually
brown hair, sometimes blonde,
behind the marrow, lies thoughts

of penance that digs and widens
the crevice of perception
deeper and deeper
—

at times of stagnant intimacy,
intimacy that redefines ephemeral,
retrospected notions replay
and stain the mind of
women,
usually brown hair,
sometimes blonde
—

by this time
he rode the wrinkles
on the bedsheets too far
destined to temporarily
subside the loneliness,
only to find out in the present
that the destination reached
has a population so nullified
that where he came from
was far better off.

House Of Wax

candle essences portraying the room
as a waxed out sort of gloom —
flickering inconstancies shadowing the
wall with silhouettes as inconstant seas
swaying the milky wall with an undertow
that invites the paint in my mind
to drip leaving a revelation to rewind
to every broken dream, every time you
reached out and felt fingertips slip
with a handle so tight yet no reflecting grip —
thoughts to paper leave the
keyboard clicks echoing a room
compressing notions in a waxed out
sort of gloom.

<u>X</u>

comfort was a long road that came to a dead end
abruptly,
happiness and companionship
left suddenly with the clutch of solace.
he was left standing there in the rain,
all senses disdained,
a seeing man now blind to ease,
seeing the fellowship of someone that ties knots in
your throat; turns your obscurities to seize.

distraught

at this very moment the quest for clenches
to console surrounded him with the ignorance
his state of mind was unable to control,
seeking and searching began in the bedsheets,
he found loneliness and
regret; mistake after mistake, temporary impassion
chose what risks to take,
drowning in seas of
duvets, suffocation on the stench of
frictional flesh and smothered in the salinity
pasted on each other's skin like the war paint of
ephemeral happiness, he searched down an
unsearchable road and lost his direction in the

orgasms; forever ringing his ears with regret. each
kiss
down
his neck, each bite to his lip, each face-blanketing
exhale, he repents with the ignorance of finding the
will to live and love between
the legs of someone who
feels the same way,
the crimson crevices carved in his back
drip with remorse and
sullen; hoping for once to leave the
bedsheets and find an
unawakened bundle of coiffure
and serenity and not calamities
of regret and sexual suicide.

Fifty / Fifty

you're the oxygen in my lungs
when they're screaming for air,
yet you're my physical pain
and my emotional despair

you're the food to my famine
when my stomach is aching,
but you're the salt to my wound
when my heart is breaking

you're the pen to my paper
when my voice runs dry,
yet you're the spark of the lighter
when the page burns high

and when my life is seized,
with hopes before you,
my burden will end
and you can start anew.

Shakespeare

at 16 they taught u
s about shakespea
re, how? but now I
realize there was m
ore learned than bl
ank stares at teache
rs waiting for bells
to slide departures
under the doors of
blank minds. balco
ny preachings in fr
ont of loveless tang
ents foreshadowing
the curvature of the
then mindless. 5 ye
ars gone I still find m
yself wandering aim
lessly to the next cla
ss with the thought o
f the useless priors a
nd the books are get
ting heavier.

Ribbon Lady

we drank and
she said I
smelled
like cigarettes
I never rubbed
her feet
but I knew
they were cold,
she was high
in heels
she left
and I
felt the
breeze
paint the
walls when
the door
slammed,
I watched
her walk
to the street
her hair
was like
stripped ribbon
it was late
and I was tired
and I woke
to a nasty

message
on the machine
but made
breakfast like
any other day.

Pinot Grigio

I'm drinking
out of
the bottle
on a tuesday
and I have
to piss
but I'm
glued to
this chair
and the keys
are glued
to my fingertips.
the room smells
like cheep wine
and fresh
duvets
I can't seem
to leave
but I always
find a way to.

Sixteen-Year-Old Girl

her innocence is soluble
when dipped in
expectations,
her mirror;
like the bottom
of dinner plates,
her wrists are
tire marks on
gravel roads,
she sees not
what we see
but in what he
sees is what
she cares,
but who is he
now?
a riptide splitting
face paint
saturday nights,
veins of toxins,
staring at roadkill
and streetlights
and garbage
hugging curb-sides
mixed with dust,
days followed
with headaches
and remorse of

dying not,
I can see it in her
eyes and
she's only 16.

Drip Noir

she's an asylum,
her walls drip blackness,
writing every word
that neglected
to slip past her
teeth,
she sleeps on
piss-stained spring
mattresses as the
cold tiles bite
at her heels,
hair and skin hide
beneath her fingernails
as palms twinge,
the padded walls
whisper screams
of coercion; wrists
bound by silence and
tightened by insanity
to bedposts
rusted,
her hands retired on
ridged thighs
hugging her
goosebumps with
convulsions of agitation,
her mind
scratches melodies of an

insomniac,
the flickering lights choke
her vision and blind her speech,
a room of contradictions
irregulating regularities
intoxicating sobriety
hallucinating reality,
the muffled screams
that weave through
the fibres of the
pillow clinched tightly
in her lap harmonize
algorithms that pull
each padded wall
towards her body
and a scream — centrefold the room,
as the walls hug her body
she awakes and paints
antonyms to
perpetual despondency.

Cigarette Cuts

he had low-grade
tattoos on his neck
and his clothes
wore transparency,
beneath his eyes
held a dying sun,
he spoke in thanks
and respect, the cuts
upon his wrists
reached a finger out
and called my eyes
to say hello,
he spoke in gratitude
for the smoke I gave him,
he smelled like cigarette
stained couch cushions
and he spoke a respectable
ebonic intellect,
his fingernails
were unswept
floor trim
and his teeth
were smashed
dinner plates
at his mother house,
departing he said
thank you
and I offered him

a cigarette for the road
and he refused and said
"for talking to me".

V.V (In Memory)

as the reflection of the trees roll off the
shined roof of the hearse I follow to the
cemetery, my mind becomes scattered
with the thoughts of our last moments.

a face so sodden,
her hand to mine, my body seized with
a contemptuous blanket of emotional
disdain, a person I loved, a person I
trusted, snatched out of my life as
fast as she changed it.
her barren body clinging on to life sent
chills up the very arms latching on
to the hospital bed, shaking, with
the thought of denial ruining every
hopeful aspect of my mind.
  this
  can't
  be
  happening,
I stare at her urn, sitting atop her
now entirety; the quiet whispers of
the funeral priest echo about the
walls in my mind, everything is silent,
white noise consumes my thoughts,
I'm shutting down, the ringing in my
ears is slowly overtaking the cries
of the siblings, the mothers, the fathers,

the cousins, and all of the friends whose lives she
truly impacted, my eyelids bare weight,
my sight is becoming dull, and the tears
are building up as the content sobs are
becoming more and more copious with
each sympathetic clutch on my shoulder,
I say my final goodbyes as we make our
way out, I whisper reverence
as a blind man
attempting to feel colours.

I touch your urn,
that's all I can
say for what you've done for me and how
you gave perspective to tunnelled vision,
the cars weep in unison departing the cemetery
with the trees spinning the roofs
after 11 shots of whiskey with
your other nephew
and with that comes a habituated
sadness.

I slip into bed, knowing that 5 miles away
there will be an empty bedside next to a
man whose life revolved
around her, a lonely
man, a broken man,
a pillow she laid her
head on not 24 hours prior, the scent of her
body; still embedded in the sheets he now
uses to wipe aside his tears,
satin sheets

enticing the walls
inward

why you?
why not me?
thoughts of abstract
painted to a pillow
eight hours I'll lay my head stagnant;
sleep not,
to the morrow, I awake
and you nevermore,

paradise may you rest.

Seattle To Syria

awakened by the
offspring's cry,
baby powdered
morning dew
showers the room,
coffee stained smiles
shine about
cheerio blanketed
kitchens,
so worrisome
for office tardiness,
the car seat won't lock
into place,
tire marks on
freshly paved driveways,
to daycare tears dry not,
she's on time,
fatigued she plants
her seed to the office seat
to grow even less
awaiting to see the smile
of her child and say
her prayers before
falling asleep.

awakened by the
offsprings cry,
gun powered
morning dew
showers the village,
rotted teeth smile
amongst the
body-blanketed township,
so worrisome of finding
a slain mother
sister
brother
just like father,
the gun won't lock
into place,
they never will,
tattered couches
paved with the
vomit of
slaughtered buildings,
mother's dead —
tears dry not,
fatigued,
hands of
grungy drainpipes
plant beside,
holding stagnant
a somber sibling,
tremors ripple
crimson tides,
planted to
grow even less
awaiting to see

the smile of
his mother
his father
his sister
and say his prayers
with brother
before laying down alone.

Dear god

dear god, I'm an unbeliever,
if there was a higher power
I don't think you'd let me leave,
you'd think the power you held would
allow you to come out from hiding
being the veil of what you claim to be
and the honesty extends beyond me,
I'm not speaking with any selfishness
only with selflessness to guide me
away from your declarations of
mandations that mold foundations
for nations that struggle under your hand,
it's all part of "god's plan", only if
the blueprints call to stand and watch
everyone crumble beneath the cries
to higher powers while the darkness pours
and showers, soaking sanity and the ignorance
of humanity.

dear god, I'm an unbeliever
I'm writing to an entity,
a supposed supreme deity
foreshadowing naive spontaneity
for those who have no one else,
I hate writing on the topic of self,
but the constant lack of health
brings not an illness
but a stillness in progress,

I'll pick up the gun cock it,
I'll fill my body with pills
and begin to rock it,
and will there be a hand to halt?
no, only a finger to point fault,
any god, any being wouldn't let sadness
flow through a spineless body,
whether a monotheistic mantra
moralizes a mental mantle or
a polytheistic point towards a
pleasant prefixed phase of
past problems postpones
the present's purity,
I'm writing to a transparent
inexistent foster parent
letting me cross the road
without looking both ways,
so, dear god, if you see this
let me count my life
in years, not days.

Ignorance Redefined, Twice

ignorant; not a care in the world (~)

holy socks drag on cracked sidewalks
she had a pink shirt,
or what seemed like it was once pink,
she wore a smile and talked to her friend,
I never saw him, but I'm sure he's nice,
I swear, her jeans never came with holes,
she's too young to sport that fashion,
her face was the moon, not the cheesy one,
but pale & distant,
her hair, matted and knotty like dad's unused
twine ball sitting in his toolbox,
did she have a brother?
where was he?
I'm sure that unclothed barbie in her hand needed a
ken

(~)

reclined with their hands
dangling over ashtrays,
where the only entity in
their mind calling for their attention
is a liver-punching depressant.
where eyes open for another hit,
and close to the cries of their children
tonka trucks make

snow angels in ash covered carpets,
walls inhale secondhand sadness;
stained with the tears of neglect,
unmade beds and unfolded
clothes shower their unpaid apartment,
eviction notices pinned to the fridge with
crayon drawings of "daddy",
her request for another beer echoes the empty room
& it crosses her mind

"where the fuck is she?".

Positivity

I was asked

    why don't you
      write something
        positive?

positive?

maybe it's like
school,
it's hard to weave
interests into subjects
you can't weave your
mind into,

a page is an unworn
white t-shirt
that I seem to stain
unrecognizable
when my pen
wipes its fingers ,

and there's nothing
more to clean my
hands with

so I guess
why I don't write

positives a majority
of the time
is because when it rains
the ground doesn't
just decide to stay dry.

The Door To Hell Is Welcoming

the entrance to my mind
portrays an appealing demeanour,
but with a glance at the contents,
portrays an intervenor
towards the progression
of anything consolingly
appeasing

or so I think

I keep pushing and
pushing until mist to dry,
a view to my loneliness
through a myopic lens
depicts nothing but self
at the following end,
a nearsighted perspective
allowing self-consciousness
to transcend into an abyssal
crevice leaving nothing but
self-blame scattered about
the exiting footprints

retrospect; permitting
history to foreshadow the
ending of every attempt
to let someone in,

I allow the spark to
grow to a flame,
putting it out in
attempt to prevent
and circumvent the
burning of the
one not to blame

the cancer in my
veins ignite with
every attempt to fight
for instances where I'm
not to blame
for instances where the
outcome is sane,
a love born a king and
deceased a slave,
a love resurrected,
mirroring death the same

the entrance is an inhaled cigarette,
that with intent and clear skies,
paints the walls, dripping with benzine
illustrating their egress as
an opposing objective to
the goal in attaining peace
by companionship.

High Hopes (Pt. I & II)

well, I'm sitting here drunk again, alone,
I remember when I was younger
I spewed disgust for those
who resorted to the bottle
as a release from their problems,
yet now I'm at the marrow of
the little boy's vision,
another sip tightens the grip
of the bottle
or the glass
depending on whether or not
I want whiskey or beer
it's usually both,
I had such high hopes for my future
now my hopes are devoted
to wondering if I have enough
money the next pack of smokes
or case of beer

       it's usually both.

   (II)

I don't even have
any social networking
site to sift through,
the internet is down,
maybe that's a good thing,

but lack of mental occupation
clutches my impotence towards
thinking good thoughts
or not even thinking at all,

there's music playing and a drink beside me
I don't even need to write that there's
a drink beside me anymore, it's usually a
given now.

I've finally altered the
definition of "achieved"
from optimistic to pessimistic
in the sense that I have
attained the task
of proving every simplistic
childhood aspiration wrong.

a 10-year-old boy, looking at himself
now would only surface denial or disgust

it's usually both.

A Whimsical Blue

fixation forces your
nails to carve my back into
an abstract painting of
the way your breath
holds my face in its grasp,
the way your
legs tighten up as they
clash to mine,
your eyes tell stories
of how your
hair wrapped to my
fingertips pulls your head
back with eyes
blank, storylines
consisting of
the surfaced portions
screaming a crimson
cry to the hands that
caress your throat,
bearing the heat
of the constant
conflict between
your skin and mine,
whispered screams of
wanted foreshadowing
allows for bodies to
convulse at signs of
complete puncture,

vocal chords tear at
points of orgasm,
a sudden bodily
shudder, bringing vibrations
to the very being pushing
your walls
to a climaxed halt,
teeth tear a chest to a skin's
stretching point,
the blood
dripping down
forefront is
the morning dew
falling off an abandoned
bed frame,
tangible exhales
hit the walls,
the walls that house
the sweaty palms of
your hands as the consistent
tremors vibrate
the bed posts, expelling
tedious creeks,
waves of warmth
clash to the walls as
my fingernails
find a homaged
home amidst the
warmth of your arms
followed by nothing more
then a shared laugh and
sudden heavy breathing.

Quitter

I should really
quit smoking her,
I'm ignorant
no more,
ashtray's
fill faster
then my lungs,
quietly whispering
tip toes provoke
the screams of
hardwood
every night
at around 1 o'clock,
making a way
to attempt quiet
openings of
neglecting doors,
sitting amidst the
tranquility as
the facial
fissure eats
the dancing smoke
while she
paints abstracts
on teeth
tongue
lungs
heart

and the
cognitive inability
to separate
index from middle
comes not from
ignorance
but from how
she holds me
tighter than anyone,
touches my lips
more compliantly
than any woman,
she will never leave me
even as I take her
top off and
share breaths,
her touch is
recognizable
most nocturnally,
I know the damage
she does to me
she'll cut my life in half,
she's the only thing
I will let in that will
kill me,
she moulds
leisure and pleasure
as if I wear them on
my back,
her body is pale
as my fingers
drip down
and feel

as I exhume
her insides
intertwining
with mine,
listening to your
cries as I inhale
provokes me to
do so more
and more
and more
until I leave you
for the night.

Shadow Self

I'm followed by a shadow
figure within the dark
of who I use to be
and am today,
reflecting in mirrors
are strangers with
crooked teeth,
late at night he
whispers memories
of a twisted body
beneath frayed rope
or sometimes
holds pictures of
walls painted with
repulsive remedies
delivered
by a bullet,
he showers skull
fragments of
suicide and kin,
I always try and shake
them off of me
I can't, it's tearing holes
in my skin
I try to pick
them off, I fucking can't,
he never lets me forget,
I'm trying to sleep,

he finds loopholes
in releases and
picks at calloused
hands watching
the dead skin rain
and dampen
rotting fresh,
he's in my dreams,
he sends faceless
apparitions
applauding something
I've done
or haven't done,
I don't know,
he shakes babies
and laughs
waking me in
cold sweats
he tells me to forget how
to breathe,
your lungs are useless
your lungs are useless
your lungs are useless

good morning.

Let Life

open wide, take the barrel, caress the lips
let the trigger be something
that's figured afterward
as one thing held by
the stress of life.

let the burden of breathing
take the wind and dwindle
the passion you have left
to rekindle your passion to live,
reloading the rifle
reviving every spiteful
feeling edging you closer to
the side of the high rise
in malevolence disregarding
the benevolence of why
you're still sitting here
reading this; ignorance to bliss.

let the goodwill of life foreshadow
that every stroke brings deep to shallow
letting life take the noose and tighten
until you loosen and righten
every wrong.

let life bring your cuts to a heal
so that you know every human can feel

a pain get better and watch the weather
go from dark skies to milky clouds dripping light
and have the poor weep, then sing together.

so let life strife your feelings of self
so that you hear the whisper from
the storm pass,
and open your eyes,
don't let the precedent of today
dictate the incident of
a familiar tangent,
because with every feeling of pain
is followed by compassion of
the morrow.

She Never Told Me Why

she never complained
about how long my hair was
or that how it reeked of
cigarettes when she kissed me
good morning,
she never painted
my skin grey
when the sun
shined,
she never told me
that my
breakfasts of
turkey sandwiches
and pepsi weren't healthy,
she told me once that
I should quit smoking
because she did,
I never did,
she says I drink too much,
she told me that
she loved me
when I made her laugh,
her legs were always warm
and I told her she could start a fire
when she doesn't shave,
she laughed,
she told me that
she loved me when

my friend died,
she never told me
why she loved me,
she never gave
me a reason to leave,
I never told myself why
she loved me, I never knew,
so I gave myself a reason

so through tears
she told me
to go fuck myself.

Near Death Last October

the past isn't something
to forget about,
she has blonde hair,
she complains about it,
always putting it up or down,
she's indecisive,
before the opaque
and past lovers,
things were
going great,
bringing up the past
like it was yesterday
or a month ago,
they kept to each other
but the tension screamed
and snapped progression,
we weren't an accident
and this relationship flipped
faster than the gravel gave out
last october,
things moved fast
like last october,
we laid in inhaling
bedsheets,
I never realized
how much perfume
she put on until she left
the duvet and I finally

exhaled,
every time we fucked
seemed like
we've been doing
it for much longer,
comfortability came with
the amount of time
the cigarettes couldn't
stop talking and talking
until 8 am,
my speech held
tandems with trust
the moment we
saw eye to eye,
retrospected reflections
given with every new kiss
dripped away from her lips
striking a match with new feelings
burning the useless old,
perpetuated post-mortem
glances to discussions of
mind depth lead to understanding,
giving swine wings
and through everything
we've gone through
in short time
she still has a
hard time figuring
to wear her hair
up or down,
and the same
with her conscience.

2 Fortnights Since

It's sometime past midnight
on a wednesday,
stumbling around the
house once again,
where floorboards
cry out and I resent
everything I said
and held back,
every cigarette
that whispered
until my lungs
turned black,
shards of beer
labels collide
with dust piles,
ashes skidded
aimlessly on
the pine,
hopelessly wandering
looking into hindsight
was only a mess to
clean up,
I haven't eaten today
but the dishes are dirty,
it's 11:30
and I'm glued
to the bedsheets
as the bed weeps

with each toss and turn
comes contemplation
to cross and burn every
memory embedded,
the bedroom smells
like cloudy ashtrays
and things unfinished,
our paths crossed
and yesterday was
tough on everyone.

Empty & Unfinished

It's odd sitting here with the
consistency of the toxicity
flowing through my veins,
the consecutive order is
fuelling the regularity to my brain,
every negative thought weaved
through sobriety surfaced through
every lie t

I was drinking one night and decided to write something.
Not knowing how much I drank, I literally passed out mid-piece and
woke up to this on my screen.

Road To Recovery

it's hard to bring life
back to someone who's
already a shadow suspended
by dust in sunlight,
a partially eaten heart
trailed by bloody
bread crumbs with no
start in sight,
replications of
past complications
forge a plagiarized
grin notarized by a shaky
pen on abstract paper,
bringing back to life
sand-burnt knuckles
reflecting tremors
through coils in the bottle
seems anything but feasible,
recovery and relapse are
few and far between
with a fine line that
splits at the seam
without warning,
the ice meeting
the bottom of the glass
is a slow
graze of fingernails
across chalkboards,

help seems out of reach
when the leather begins to
leech to your skin
with each question repeated
over and
over and fucking over,
perceptions of positivity
can only withhold the
constant of being
a placeholder in
the tangent of
consistencies,
but light has the ability to break
through windowsills
and curtains,
yes I speak from experience
because it's the only thing
that wakes me up in the morning,
but as I become used to
walking dead,
I found my light that
wakes me up
in the afternoon
and puts me to sleep
at night.

Like Him

I wish you loved me how
you loved him,
you speak with
reverence to memory
and not of present,
emotions run not
through your veins;
with me, at least,
it seems,
I haven't shed a tear
in 10 years yet
the lack of
sentiment lies
within you,
I feel achieved
when I hear an
"I love you",
I'm listening through
static; thinking I hear
clearly but being drowned
out by what's louder,
your touch is deafening
to clarity, and I don't know
if they felt this way too,
reaching out to transparency
never seemed so tangible,
and being grazed by
fingertips of yesterday never

felt so confusing,
your emotion seems
only soluble through
my tears, and my tears
only seem to fall
with your emotion.

I wish you loved me
like you loved him.

Cardinal's Cry

sure,
I need to
stop drinking
and stop
smoking but
when bad habits
become consistencies
that let you
survive the nights,
the ability to
shake the
rusty smell off
the fibres on your
back become
a bookmark,
one that prevents you
from turning the page
in a fear driven
halt of wondering
what happens next,
the stench that
trails through
teeth to nose
is a tail to
a comet that won't
burn out,
the embers of each
cigarette that kisses my lip

burn out like previous
feelings towards past lovers,
I was in a state
of loving memory of
having love and memories,
until a therapeutic graze
of absolution picked me up
and brushed the bruises off
the bottom of my feet
given by
stomping the ominous
solitary of rock bottom
so many fucking times,
I still drink
and I still smoke
but when a
tedious whisper
tells you to stop
hurting and stop
hating when hurt
and hate is all you've
felt for moonlight
exceeded,
you can't just pick
the scars off of your
skin and liver
and walk past mirrors
without urges of
cardinal knuckles
and tremors coexisting,
I wish to stop
like you tell me to,
I wish washing my clothes

would dredge the stench
of yesterday clean,
but maybe the pain
of the past is stained on
my skin and
not my clothes.

5 Days

I haven't felt her
in 5 days,
I haven't felt
how delicate
the rim of her
mouth feels
against mine,
how enticing it
is to get a taste,
I have to taste
all of her,
they way she
flows through me,
she mends all that's
broken, then breaks
it when she leaves,
it's only been 5 days,
I miss the bitter taste,
the way she makes
my tongue curl
up like a slug
swallowing tablespoons,
she pulls me in,
and hangs me with
the rope she yanked,
scraping the bottom
of the barrel
for even a scent of what

will remind me of her,
every taste
is like losing my
virginity for
the last time,
and she became
so much more
than a past-time,
so much more than
something to
pass time,
it's been 5 days,
soon to be back
at the crack of the
new year,
she's a constant
resolution
that I can't wait
to break,
or is it me *she* can't
wait to break,
she leaves a bitter taste
on my mind
and the thoughts that flow
through my veins,
she's someone I can
thank, she's someone
I try so hard to forget,
she dictates and mediates,
a forged signature
on bills passed to
loved ones,
telling them that I'm okay,

but only for the night,
she's anger, she's happiness
she paints vermilion kisses
on my knuckles,
and heals crimson
crevices in my mind,
it's only been 5 days,
I'll see you soon
I'll taste you soon.

Turn Your Head

years of negativity
like seeing your
reflection on the other
side of the glass barrier,
I never looked both ways
when crossing the road
because for years
I've been blind
to anything that
came close,
waking up
felt like finding
a new strand of
cancer somewhere
every day,
I heard nothing but
voices, I knew I
was hurting myself
but I never stopped to
look both ways,
I realized it wasn't
just me that I was
impaling with sadness,
sometimes darkness
shines light on life
more than light itself
ever will,
at the bottom of

every bottle, my heart
would sit and drown until
I ended up swallowing it
back into my chest,
slowly the liquid
is veering from
being stained red,
every mirror
reflects more than just
a face, it shows a past
so dark the
background
is the focus,
instead of looking
at the rocks beneath
my feet crumbling,
I've been taking steps back,
hands like blenders
left on too long
are reaching towards
pulling the plug,
looking both ways
has always been
a problem for me,
but I finally
caught a glimpse
at what happens
to the left and realized
that change is right.

Lipstick

don't let your
lipstick wear,
if it feels the urge to,
put some more on,
if you can't find the
stick in your purse,
just try and get through
the night, the morning
will be kind,
I promise it's not
a waste of time,
don't let your
shirt drip,
don't let your
buttons wave
beneath your waist,
choose a pair that
fits tighter around
the hips,
tomorrow will be kind,
use your eyes to talk
use your eyes to deny,
use your words with me,
tell me where your
lipstick is hiding.

Smoke Filled Garage

it's late,
or early,
depends on how you
look at it,
only my hands and
heart are cold,
smoke filled garage,
rusted tools
hang themselves
in front of me,
paintless brushes
and painted brushed and
baseless screwdrivers,
ashy floors and drywall
painted with holes
from fists and hockey pucks,
church pew stools
razor-slit,
spray painted
by angsty young
I sit upon,
unfinished projects
are suppose to sit on
the other side of
the workbench.

Fiction Addiction

I've been addicted to many things,
some things better than the others,
and I have yet to categorize her.

when she left me,
I started withdrawing
the moment she stopped calling
my name to hurry up
with the sliced hot dogs,
the moment the complaints
about her tea being too cold
left the mold her voice
built inside my head,
a mold filled with
unfinished memories
cut short by good intentions
and being cracked by
tensions of mental state,
being happy on my own
was the reason and the
latter concluded at treason,
a nicotine addiction
to her; fiction,
I share both
with hope of only
shaking one,
each cigarette

I smoke I know
kills me,
every kiss,
is a gunshot not
to my lungs
but only
a feeling
that comes
and never leaves,
but my addiction
every day seems to
categorize itself
the more my heart
ends up fitting
the mold.

Amber House

the things that last
never happen overnight,
but tonight seems
to last too long,
this feeling hasn't left
me since you did,
a gut full of
"what if's"
consume my
mind into
"why didn't I's",
maybe there is someone
better off for you,
someone who
has his shit together,
who's ambition
isn't a closet of
empty hangers,
darkness doesn't
resolve on its own,
this stomach ache
of regret lingers upon hacks
and coughs,
the smoke consumes my
lungs, reaching from the
ground up,
a house beneath ashes isn't
rebuilt by the owner.

Bad Decisions Left Unforgotten

I wish it was easier for
people to forget,
if things left their
mind as easy as they let
them in, tough skin
wouldn't wear thin
as easy as it is right now,
my past is full of imperfections
and bad decisions, leaving unstitched
incisions beneath the brink of sanity,
but who's isn't?
every time falsities
start, my mind races
with my heart to contemplations on
when to finish, they tattoo the past
of others on their insecurities,
fuelling the fire that burns a hole
into respect and reputation,
creating a vicious cycle
of revenge and envy,
each gossip verbally vomited
into naive ears pulls the marionette
strings of perception into the road normally
taken, when the ignorance
burns yellow to ash, the road less taken
seems blocked, so the next time you hear
something about another, don't be too quick

to spread the word.

the game of telephone can get a
little distorted when
the next phone call
you get is that they
were found hanging from
a rope.

Chest Tattoo

your name
tattooed on
the inside of
my chest and
every time my
heart beats
it reminds me
of you.

Bird's Eye View

not sure if people keep
losing interest
or just lie to begin with,
it's hard hiding pain
with noisome eyes,
people will begin
to ask questions,
and I will begin
to answer,
after years of hiding
I find it harder and harder
to tint the truth,

yet, there's a piece of me
that's starting to realize
that it's me,
maybe interest isn't being lost,
when I let you into my mind
it's as if you coexist with my
mental state and
with correspondence
comes the thought of
reciprocative standpoints,
my hands are calloused
from pushing;
making pulling
insurmountable,
it's my mind

painting caution lines,
all I'm asking for
is a rooftop view,
staring down
with a bird's eye
view on you and I,
I'm not ashamed
of pushing, cause it's led
me to today, but I'm afraid
of continuing, cause I don't
want tomorrow
to be like yesterday,
I'm content,
and my hands
are in my pockets.

Eventide

it's a normal night,
a little bit of booze and
the sky has something
in its teeth,
I can't pick at it
all I can do is look
as it smiles down at me,
the chill peeking into my skin
as everything around me
seems so content,
raspy footsteps around
a frozen yard trickle
down my earlobes,
moonlit cigarette smoke
dancing like scissors
across my upper lip,
the sound of nothing
but tearing paper
kindling before my eyes,
distant cars singing roadside echoes,
charing my ears
like burning flower pedals,
and all that crosses my mind
is the how unfathomable
the beauty of nighttime is,
I find myself daydreaming
when the sun sets

and sleepwalking
when it rolls over,
the emptiness of
eventide is a glass
half-empty being
topped off half-full,
repressing every
ominous feeling of
daytime, but the
one thing that
will subside not
is the ubiquitous
thought of you.

Small City

I can't tell if
it's my mind or my
ash stained and burn hole t-shirts,
both can make a woman run,
the trail dust stirring
is starting to make my
skin burn, I'm starting
to learn that maybe
love isn't for everyone,
it has an acquired taste,
sometimes it takes
a plague to kindle
a sense of realization
but I've solely realized
that one can only die
so many times before
love settles with the dust,
I thought only my lungs were
black but I guess when
you're that close to the heart
the pain is bound to rub off,
my chest is wet eraser
scribbling over a dry pencil-written past,
falling in love seems to be a falsity,
everything ends,
lit like a small city
but you can see the smog
from a mile away,

stop coming to visit,
you're not welcome.

<u>To Kin</u>

thus far I've lived a
pretty care-free life,
disregarding consequences
like a bee sting,
I want you to watch
my footsteps,
look at the direction
they went, don't see if your
foot fits, it's not a hard
path to mold,
I see potential,
you make 20/20
unequivocal,
transpicuous youth
floats over my skin
like it was yesterday,
your eyes tell stories of
pain, it scares me to
even see a diminutive
of myself in you,
you absorb like
cigarette smoke hugging
cotton sweaters,
and exhaling burdens
to your skin,
you define rarity,
your clarity will come soon,
don't give up,

your road is endless,
don't veer,
in your horizon
the sun never sets unless
you pull it down
and you've been in
the dark for so long,
you live and love with
the lights off,
you can't see the tread
that I've learned to
dread with your head in
the sand, open your
blinds and let the sun
trickle in and heal your scars,
it's waiting for you,
the mirror you look in
is distorted on your
own grounds,
I look in the same
mirror every time
I open up photo albums,
looking at your ice cream
stained blouses smiling
with mom,
you might not know
but I look at those
pictures more than
you think,
your millstone eyes
showed as life
grew grey hair,
your despair isn't

tattooed, but my past is,
look at my footfall
and read my eyes,
my cumbersome
direction is a
tough pill to swallow
and where I am
there's no water
to wash it down.

*To Hannah, my blood, my sister, my best friend.

How To Be A Successful Poet

hurt people and feel bad about it,
keep hurting people and keep
feeling bad about it,
get hurt and
don't be resilient,
wallow.

make beer your
only companion,
fuck a lot,
play the piano
on your thighs
when you're stressed,
tap your feet,
it's going to sound terrible
and that's okay,
you'll get used to it,
tremors will send
pain to your veins
like broken tea bags.

don't sleep,
eat terribly,
put turkey on
bread and keep
the skin on,
hurt and feel bad,
know you'll keep hurting

and keep fucking,
keep drinking,
read your mistakes
bookmark them,
you'll keep coming back,

smoke cigarettes and
don't cry,
fear death only when
you're dead,
and have a thin wallet,
there's no such thing
as a rich poet,
cause we're all
broken in some way.

Worn Lipstick

she ran red lipstick over
her fingertips before she
ripped out his heart
to give it colour,
she put it back, mind you,
I can't say she broke it,
I can't even say she ripped it out,
it was involuntary,
he gave it to her,
and the thought of
rejection made him
take it back,
an unfinished
cigarette put back in the pack
and lit later,
nothing tastes the same,
bitter almost,
she set fire to it
and ran from the smoke,
she came back once it all settled,
and all that's left is ash,
she always catches him saying
"sorry this my last one"
but he'd let her smoke him empty,
his heart is still red and
the lipstick has worn,
and that's what made him realize
that she's the one.

Broken Statu(r)e

the broken can break even more,
a piece of shattered glass
can always splinter
into smaller pieces;
they hurt more to step on,
rock bottom is only
a paradox,
I've never met an end
of hopelessness,
a blade of grass can only
sway until it's been cut,
and I'm trimming myself,
I've been trimming myself
the entire time,
at once I thought life was being lifted,
and nothing that's held high stays high,
arm's begin to tire,
I once viewed sunsets
and skylines as timelines
to progress,
I now only reminisce,
the repetition of worn
down faces and barren
chest spaces show me
that every mirror
is double sided,
and the reflection in which
I once confided

now spits in my face,
when I was young
I thought I could withstand
being a broken man,
I could never see the echo of
my eyes in the hourglass and
I was too young,
too young to understand
that it was a problem, but now
it's tipped on its side and
I'm itching at the sand on my skin.

The End Of Something That Never Really Began

your eyes are different,
I've written about eyes
in the past,
I've been metaphorical but
not genuine, I miss your eyes
even when they're staring at me,
they have this ambiguity,
they're grey clouds,
sometimes they rain,
and they hide the sun,
I've never seen anything like it,
I know you're broken,
there are secrets hiding
behind your teeth,
I know your eyes tell stories,
I've tried to read,
but you keep forcing me
to bookmark,
every time,
everything is primitive;
a tangible omega, always,
I'd like to feel I've
been in love before,
but your eyes are different,
they write scriptures on napkins,
they burn so easily.

I Always Write Like This At Night

I'm still in awe at the fact
that I can stand straight,
I can't tell if I'm mindless
or spineless, whenever I'm
asked to leave, I leave,
I never slam the door,
when I'm asked to come back
I drop what I'm doing and knock,
the door isn't always answered
and that's what picks away
at my backbone,
I stay planted
on the same doormat I've
tainted with leaving footprints,
steadfast shinsplints are nails on
chalkboards,
I keep running,
but you know I'll be back,
so keep that doormat clean.

Seventeen

a child covered in
animated scum brought
up by the creator's tongue,
buried down through growth
by hands that feed,
her self-confidence
is a rose under
suffocating weeds,
crawling their way
up her arms,
misfortune is a
pernicious gift;
not being able to
choose family,
she's owned at
seventeen,
striving for an
evergreen family tree,
but stuck under a willow,
with only a pillow
to gather rain,
her clean water
only comes from the pain
that the wind brings in,
blowing palms painting
imperfect skin,
she's a tangible truth

but a verbal fiction,
telling stories of what
she wished happened,
but for now
she's a product of
forenoon resentment,
with endless time spent
under the willow tree
watching the leaves
trickle their way through
the sands of time,
until she turns eighteen,
counting sheep,
and at only seventeen
she's too sore to sleep.

Vicegrip

I'm sorry for wearing your
shoulders down,
for wearing a rusted crown this entire time,
for disguising this threadbare throne,
I promise I'll make every
burden of yours my own,
I've said you've ran away
and I've held it against you,
there's no haste,
I understand,
I've seen it second to you
and thirdhand,
and instead of servitude
I see aptitude,
you will escape,
sometimes instead of
pulling through the vice grips
you have to spin the other way,
I understand.

there's nothing vain
in putting your pain before,
you've stopped running
yet when trouble tramples
as hard as it has,
the footprints are in cement.

it's easy turning a blind eye

to a mirror when the reflection
is a projection seen before,
I'll stay tight in vice
and keep my laces loose.

O're Is the Whore Of Tomorrow

It is as it is,
and was ere,
again I'm paired to
restroom pantile,
resilient sickness
can redefine docile
to nothing northerly,
o'er the day is
only forgery
to a nightly
mainstay,
this white flag
has been waving
to porcelain for
oft fortnights
shining footlights
on an innocent reflection,
allay this suffocation,
let me breathe again,
foremost is always
surviving tomorrow,
though I'm a swain to
the whore of today.

The Liveliness Of Night Helps Me Forget The Inertia Of Day

I've been questioned on
my late night walks,
why do I do it?
the repetitive cracks
sing hedonistic soliloquies
at every avoidance,
the streetlights eat away
at forfeiting darkness,
vomiting garbage cans
spew synthetic carrion
and winking storefronts
seduce nightfallers,
trash kissing curbs
pushing away affection
cry out for help,
cigarette butts cloud
sandy sidewalks
and hug dragging soles,
passing cars and
mindless youth
spewing timeless
nothings out car windows,
cop cars and crisis topped
middle-agers stumbling their way
to fast food and
regretful forenoons,
I've been questioned

on where I'm walking to,
but never what I'm walking from,
no matter where I go,
I find myself
burning my throat
with coffee at 2 am.

Seven Dollar Tip

I'd love to find myself a suit, drive twelve minutes
and sit on a barstool that won't stop screaming. Be
able to smoke inside again, piss in cocaine stained
toilets. Push on locked stalls and trip over high heels
that reach out from under like ashes ready to be
flicked. Have makeshift conversations with a sixty-
two-year-old bartender who throws an ashtray and a
glass of jack on the bar rail at the same time every
day and who spurns at irregulars. Harlequin nods at
pseudos and tire at denial to another. Pay a $13 cab-
fare and let him keep a 20 for listening to me bitch
about how I should be able to smoke inside the cab
like "the good old days". Find myself questioning
every single piece I've ever written while spinning
beneath my sheets, wake to work and work 'till 5, I
don't yearn for much just a kiss for when I leave and
one when I come home, if she's still up.

Known Stranger

I want to meet myself as if I've never tried to understand myself. Run into him at a party, drunk, at 3 am hearing what he's fucked up, and how he misses youth and hates cancer and himself. I want to watch him writing at coffee shops and contemplate saying hello because he looks like he wants to die. I want to bump into him on the subway and apologize, I want to pick apart his mind, stand awkwardly beside him at a crosswalk, listen to his cross-talk and how he refuses to capitalize god's name when he writes about him. Watch as he writes this piece and tries to understand why he wants to understand himself so badly that he'll stand at his own funeral, being his own shoulder, wishing he could slide out of his own shoes.

Run On

if you put me in a cage
would I be a rat or a petition?

would you sign it or
watch until the screams you
can't listen to
my cries for help
me save me and
give me the key
to life is fighting
through the
bars and pubs
are nothing but a vice
grip tied tight to the
bricks that can't wipe
the cement from its eyes
tell the stories that eat
at the chipped away skin
covered in spiders
digging to the core
of the earth is wrapped in
expectations and relation
ships sailing with no sail,
manless and handless
mannequins reaching out for
help confined by my vein
minds and empty hearts
are suppose to carry love,
at least that's the perception

that I cant pull to conception
built on deception with exception of
reception's inception,
a look inside my mind
your own fucking business.

Why Don't You Write A Book? (Irony)

"why don't you write a book?"

they'll expect
a second,

if consistency
and money
was consistent
see, I'd write a book,

poetry is a dying art,
you'll find a needle
every now and then
but the hay is bound
together with cellphones
and bongs
and unexpected
suicides,

no one wants to hear
how sleep deprived you are
because your sheets feel
like moth wings
and how your skin
feels like
a burning painting,
why cigarettes kiss
harder and how love

feels like the bottom
of a dinner plate,

you'll find compassion
and understanding
but finding a diamond in
the rough is
only valuable if
you can escape.

The Worst Thing I've Ever Done Was Letting The World Know I Write

the worst thing I've ever done
was letting the world
know that I write,
it's not the 2 am phone calls
asking if I'm okay,
it's not the regret
of relationships or
the running away,
it's the look in my mothers
eyes when I write about dying,
it's the regard to kin
when holding certain
emotions in,
forging positivity
and relaying
the antiquities
of struggle,
the minuscule
moments of will
drill into minds
painting all kinds
of doubtful abstracts,
creating spousal transacts
of how to fix their son,
it's not the questions
about what I mean when I
say my skin spits goose flesh

or my eyes wrap yesterday
in spruce mesh that
eventually frays,
it's the days where
I get kindred
phone calls
wondering if I'll pick up
because of my piece
the night before
stating that
I'm skating
on thin ice,
I don't want them to worry
I'll be fine,
but for now, it's the pen
that has to unwind
the noose from
confining words
I refuse to say.

Falling In Love With A Writer

If you enjoy having every fibre of your
consciousness picked apart by literary vomit at 2 am
on a Wednesday,
Fall in love with a writer.

If you enjoy fighting over incorrect grammar usage,
Fall in love with a writer.

If you want to constantly have your eyes rolled at
every time you question a metaphor,
Fall in love with a writer.

If you want to be swept off your feet and then
promptly put back down in the same piece of
writing,
Fall in love with a writer.

If you want to feel worried when the phone isn't
answered,
Fall in love with a writer.

Mood swings and sleepless nights?
Fall in love with a writer.

If tangible expression conveys unequivocal
compassion,
most of the time, don't fall in love with a writer.

If you want to misinterpret pieces of writing
because of the uncertainty of the author,
Fall in love with one.

If you find that yesterday you were in love with a
completely different person, if you find that your
skin is often referred to as porcelain cigarette ash, if
your eyes are viewed like the first time you saw two
flies fucking, if the lump in your throat lives on
ballpoints, you've fallen in love with a writer.

There's no turning
back at this point,
falling out of love
with a writer is like
saying goodbye to a
phone with no dial tone.

Colourant Sheets

I'm tired of the past,
the decisions I made,
tenfold I've expressed
the displeasure of every action,
but every fraction of pleading
is never enough to rid
minds of tattered bedsheets,
or the hues that make up
the painting I've been
trying to erase,
but these colours don't run,
and there's ink coloured umbrage
in these veins and it flows
at piqued destinations,
sitting behind eyes
that see too well,
today, I know will
eventually become the past,
but I've been trying to
drag the pigment
of yesterday into something
tomorrow won't look back on,
and tow a sodden eraser
over wet ink,
I can promise that
I've changed and
nowhere in the book

written by regret
does it say
that anyone will believe me,
and I'm beginning
to accept that,
every day I have to stare
at intangible scars left
by blades tipped
with foretimes
and the ringing of
these wind chimes are becoming
white and I'm getting tired,
it's putting me to sleep
and I've given up on
counting sheep because
the breeze of attempting to
forget my past is soothing enough,
these colours don't run,
and I wonder if tomorrow
I'll wake up in colourant sheets.

Sorry Mom

I still live with my parents
and at 2 am I walk around
the house with cum-stained
boxers and drink
caffeinated drinks,
when I drink, I drink,
when I run out of money
I drink my parents' booze,
I smoke and my dad
fucking hates it,
I can barely afford it,
I work 3 times a week if I'm lucky,
and buy clothes I don't need,
and food I shouldn't eat,
I bitch about religion
on social networking
sites and I dropped out
of going to university,
I want to be a writer,
I still live at home with
my parents,
are the two synonymous?
my sister is 17,
18 in december,
and she's going to school
for the love of darwin
stick with it
don't be like your brother,

I know I have a kind heart
and cry when my tire eats roadkill
but compassion doesn't pay the bills,
I can sit here and personify my life
as dragging a worn sock full of pebbles
down the street and giving a sock to myself
as a gift for someone who wanted pebbles
but I'm not going to anymore,
factualities sanded down
into some form of actualities
that resemble anthology,
I am by no means dumb,
my comprehensive abilities
are above average, I know I could
have gone through school
with ease, for christ's sake
I was taking english literature,
I sure use a lot of religious expletives
for a sickened nihilist,
regardless of the fact,
my boxers are dry now.

It's Been A While

I haven't been
drinking much lately,
I haven't wrote
anything in a while,
and I always knew
putting the two
hand in hand was never fine,
a healthy vice is trapped
by an unhealthy outlet,
and the curious kid looking
for a spark
had dried his fork,
I do miss the teeth sinking
into my throat,
having the pain
run to my hands,
I miss waking up
with cinderblocks
glued to my scalp,
the nightstand used to eat
up the empty bottles
and the stomach pains are
now keeping me up at night,
I remember whiskey stained
chest hair and biting at hangnails,
bloody fingers and the
taste was fuel,
I remember writing

and waking up
and erasing
and waking up,
what is a poet?
I'm going to have
a drink and this was
written sober.

A Mirror & A Casket

the result of my previous work
you've read is not something
that has just flowed down a
current of creativity, don't be fooled,
the amount of wasted words wilted,
stuck to wine stained cedar desks and
lost in distraction of cigarette smoke
and the blood of a workdays fist,
the open windows
on a computer of
unfinished work
is only proof that I can see
a reflection in the screen
when it's turned off too,
the lament of the mouse
and the little red x
turns the clicking
into grinding teeth,
oh, yes..
sometimes I can write a piece in minutes,
but other times, I'm either rekindling a
relationship of drywall and knuckle,
pouring drinks,
lighting cigarettes,
answering phone
calls, coughing through
fields of wet cement
in my throat,

or staring at the paper as
a mirror in a casket,
when I sit down and write
with cigarettes and drinks
the outside world doesn't exist
but at the same time
reality has never
existed as much as it has
at that moment.

Priorities

I'm staring through cigarette smoke,
having a drink of rum and coke
listening to an 8-minute Periphery song,
an in-depth conversation,
the ticking of typing,
patio lights
and staring
into nothing
in between stanzas
I'm humming alone,
and tapping my feet,
it's 1:09 am
and I work at 6 am,
morning fatigue
can get on its knees.

The After Midnight Bird

I told her she reminds me
of a bird chirping at 1 am
and she never asked why,
strange yet beautiful,
inconsistent and seldom,
appreciative upon scarcity,
a hedonist of silence
has never found serenity
in the blurred lines of infinity,
but the confidence of
clamour will fade
with every night a chirp
goes unheard,
the consistency
of inconstancy is the hand
that feeds and the
bite that bleeds.

A Floating Cobweb

the aftermath of a finished
cigarette lingers in the air
and I pick at it like a
cobweb in the wind,
floating aimlessly
unable to grasp,
and I've never felt
so weightless.

After Midnight Wolf

an after midnight wolf
lives as a sheep by day,
amongst opposites
he sees through
sheep's clothing
and moralizes through
insecurities,
though inaccurate,
accusations man
a marionette,

a wolf in sheep's clothing
can manipulate but
is easy to forgive,
an after midnight wolf
can ruin his sheepskin,
and have follicles run dry,
alcohol and anger
and selfish malevolence
over compassion, thought and
apathetic benevolence,
the sun can divide strong from weak,
an after midnight wolf lashes
and drinks
and lashes,
regrets and lacks morals
yet lacks intent,
only listens to his mind

and not his heart,
he sheers himself
with broken bottles
and it takes a while
to grow back.

Bloodsucking From Eighteen On

I'm a mosquito trapped
in a clapping hand,
I know that I can be bothersome
but I'm just trying to survive.

Jealousy

I create my own jealousy,
     and load my own gun,
I make my own bed,
     I never shoot
and
     I never sleep,
I'm a stagnancy
of
imperfections,

the cement is dry now,
I'm sorry,
but you can't leave.

Diamond On Spikemoss

she saw through
my   pseudo smiles
and
empty eyes and
    gave me
iris' of blossom
and perpetuity,
if she had
    kaleidoscope lenses
she'd still see
  me
clearly,
she'll always
be my median of
perceptive mires
or
thoughtless meadows,
if a diamond in the rough
sleeps on spikemoss,
is it   still worth something?

Memory Loss

not sure if overreacting is a
sign of weakness or passion,
I lash out over little things
and shorten breaths over things
that live for little in my mind,
the violent expirations of chest
and mind saw the door frame
a little bigger every time,
regret comes after,
I'd call it short term memory loss,
with every responsibility I've taken,
steps back; I've taken two
the ratio is uncanny,
I'm starting to believe that
instead of the urge to change
I have the desire to
desire change,
the steps that follow
are getting deeper
and situations are
becoming shallow
yet my reactions
stay the same,
I've wished
and promised reversal,
the pills and reclined leather
really does nothing,
I'll swim in my vices and

the unfortunate thing
is that I know how to swim.

Banned

I'm an asshole when I drink
and the manager of the only
bar in town found that out,
I never was keen of
social drinking anyways,
everyone thinks that
drinking alone is a problem,
I think alone,
and a thought process
like mine is a lot deadlier
than liquor when left in isolation,
prioritize your worries, friends.

<u>Wind</u>

find that someone
who becomes the
gust of wind that
turns the weight
on your shoulders
to dust.

Oxymoron

life is more than
eating, drinking,
fucking, thinking
about regret, and neglect,
finding new ways to
keep the sadness
you curse every night
in your writing
to stick around,
holding addictions
to things you know
you shouldn't,
watching porn
and thinking that
your sex life is less
than ropes and
fishnets,
eating food and
smoking things
you know
you shouldn't,
saying things to loved
ones you know you
wouldn't if you were sober,
and dwelling
and never forgetting
and never forgiving
life is realization, resilience,

and repeating mistakes,
hating yourself and loving
yourself and enduring pain
embracing serenity and reading
in-between the lines,
being able to clean
dirty mirrors,
seeing reflections
in coffee, and being able
to finish it,
having ephemeral
epiphanies and going back
on your word to quit
smoking, quit drinking
and eating terrible,
being able to laugh
and cry and punch drywall
in the same day,
life is realism,
not some realm
of imaginable
perfection, you're going
to fill a glass with constant
fuck ups, just keep finishing it
and filling it with a
manifestation of manipulation
that you have no problem
seeing past,
be an oxymoron.

I'm Not A Liar

I'm not a liar
but I lie to myself,
I'm not a sociopath but
I dream of killing people,
and I know that
I'm a person at heart,
I sleep on pillows made
of memories and
listen to my own screams
and take them in as whispers,
I sleep on mattresses of
dad's smiles and yesterday,
self identified as ignorant
and educated in night,
the sun went down
on me once and
I never came.

Ash

I've been scolded at before
while smoking in front of public places,
but today she
stared at me with a
cold look and bitterness,
were you sent
to school smelling like
the couch cushions and bedsheets
and your mothers hair?
was it the ashtrays beside dinner plates
and squinted grins through dancing fog
watching television with your ears?
burning lungs and showers
and breathing with your eyes?

I'm sorry, I tried blowing smoke
the other way.

90's Grunge

I like 90's grunge that
makes me want to kill myself
and not wash my hair
and drink beer,
don't see them
live anymore,
they're old now
and it fucks you
with the bitterness
of life,
get drunk
kiss the floor
for supporting you
and lay in comfort.

Callow & Murderous (I)

I sat watching 3 girls,
couldn't be any older than 12,
wearing shorts cut by
expectations and
   taking pictures
with coffee cups and
wearing make up
stronger   than
perfume clouds
following like
hitchhikers
and
teasing cars,
smut magazines and enraptured
by the   irrelevant famous,
exposing the youth's lack
of interest in literature,
callow and murderous,
glasses filled and smug,
the world in front of them
and yet they're taking
steps backwards.

An Ocean Look

a soft voice that can
sanitize a mind, and
that mirrors skin like linen,
hair flowing faster than
blood to her heart,
looking in her eyes
proves that cerulean skies
can walk on earth,
anxiety blurs the lines
of a perfectionist,
leaving reservations
in the minds of anyone
lucky enough to
grace tangibility and
her footsteps cohere,
with lips rarely touched
a godless man can feel them
in his fingertips when praying
to a god he doesn't believe in.

I'm Not Crazy

I'm starting to come to terms
with hate and insanity,
I drove to her house at 4 am
because she wasn't answering her texts,
and I called her 30 times cause I thought
she got into a car accident,
but she was clearly
fucking someone else,
I hit a skunk just
after leaving my house at 4am
and I never smelt anything,
I've been sitting on her shoulders for
as long as we've known each other,
and all I've become is heavy dust,
I have good intentions,
but they're transparent,
my heart is consistent
but translucent,
a transient feeling of
reciprocated compassion
sparks immeasurable
inconsistencies in
sane behaviour,
but I have good intentions,
and every day we sit in a vessel
with no holes and I try to patch
them because I feel like I'm drowning,
and eventually she'll want to swim,

she turns amnesia into a theory,
she's a mirror and I'm seeing
an evolutionary reverse,
before I see clearly
I'll have to wipe the fingerprints.

This House Is Falling Apart

we built a house with our bare hands
and you moved out,
then back in and it's haunted now,
I know you have a hard time sleeping
but I've memorized every floorboard
that creaks and it sings me to sleep
every time you try and leave,
I get confused whether it's the lullaby
of coming or leaving that knocks me out,
this house began to burn and I sat for months
putting it out while you stood
there with cold feet,
and now you're warm and I'm
stuck peeling the ash off of my skin,
the grass is still green and the
picket fence is freshly painted
but apparently I used the wrong colour,
the doorbell is a muttering of
apologies and the doormat is a mirror,
the bed we slept in
hasn't been made since you left,
I'm stuck sleeping with ghosts
and brushing my teeth beside
no one to tell me that I haven't
been brushing for long enough,
I'm showering in hot water in the middle
of summer because the steam
pulls the mirror off the wall,

and all I want is for you to come back,
our house is dirty and the callouses on
my hands are starting to become smooth,
my skin is almost clear again,
please come back.

A Pessimistic Onlooker Observes The Harsh Reality Of Relationships

Today I walked about 70 metres and
saw two couples fighting in their vehicles,
the first couple stopped at a red light
and I could hear the bickering,
the child in the backseat was yanking on
the straps of the car seat like
a regretful rollercoaster, and
the only thing I saw in the reflection of
the glass was a teen drinking away
the memories, or lack thereof,
the second couple looked well off
they were driving a jet black Jeep Cherokee
and it looked well maintained, the type
to wash his car in the rain,
and his face was full of blood,
no kids, maybe they were older
and off to college but the steering wheel
took beatings and the gas pedal
cut the floor carpet into pieces,
the cause is unknown, the affect is unknown,
I sat staring into an hourglass wondering how
beautiful their first months or
maybe their first few years were,
did he sit in the bathroom
while she did her make up?
did she put on layers of interest
when he told tales of how
shitty his day was?

did he accept the concept that
girls do in fact shit a lot?
did 25 years go by quick?
or 5 for the first?
they were younger,
are they fucking right now?
or is she on the ground
or is he on the couch?
this glass of sea sick ice
will continue to tattoo
foreshadowings of minuscule information
on my fingertips, and I'll sit in wonder
all night if they're going to make it through this,
cause for now, I have no hope.

Broken Clock

bottle caps bouncing on cement floors
played in a constant loop,
cigarette ash fraying the
consistency of the tapping,
tapping and tapping on a window pane
with only rain reciprocating,
if only any of this was real,
real life is but only a momentary
manipulation of the things,
or by the things that make it easier,
a broken clock synchronized
with progression
of this silent
lunged apparition and
mobility has never been
defined by an antonym
until now,
now formalized mistakes
carve themselves
inside the walls
of a crimson tower and shine out
as the falsities of my "finest hour",
our lives are controlled by vices,
vice grips and patterned slices
solidify consistency in off-timed
8th notes that tick
tick,
tick like the broken clock.

The Devil Is I

for a man who doesn't believe in god,
I've been spoken to by the devil more than once,
he sent bullets of whiskey
cutting through my throat,
he made me realize that it's a problem
and then dug me a mote,
and he knows I can't swim,
he put pins in my skin
and glued me to a bed,
he put demons in my mind
and put happiness at the
end of a frayed thread,
he stands beside me at funerals,
and behind me in line at
forced confessions
in catholic high schools,
he washed my hands clean
of blood after breaking a heart,
he points south of finish lines
northerly of where to start,
he puts me in the shoes
of the man in the mirror,
he makes money in my
wallet disappear,
he tells me to control my anger,
then has others lay hands on the
confidence of my little sister
and puts blinds over my eyes,

he tells me tomorrow will be different,
and laughs when I call him out on lies,
he takes vacations from my brain
and brings rain when I'm parched,
then sticks his skin-peeled
fingers down my throat
and makes me vomit
out on to paper, to regret
what I wrote,
I will never pray
because to my self I won't lie,
after years of mirrors I realize
that in fact the devil is I.

Wintry Contagious

I've manifested
an after midnight symphony,
looping mp3's of my own eulogies
and consecutively callousing
and shaking hands with death,
the feeling brings a paradox of
finding warmth in cold palms
and it cuts between relation and
addiction to a palpable misery,
shot glasses of blood trying to make
home in my throat
drawing puke
and neglecting to force
warmth back inside,
left cold
and red hands ramble
abstract frigidness
on a livid mess mimicking
a sorry excuse for a heartbeat,
and all I've been doing is
touching myself
and each fingertip friction
formalizes an addiction to
a wintry contagious.

Clotheslines & Cigarettes

I used to go out for cigarettes before bed
with music and connection to the world,
I've learned now to clam the
addiction to nosiness about
trump and
syria,
petitions about
dying dogs and
sensitivity,
and I just sit out there with a shovel
in my eyes digging the other way and
appreciating the sky and watching the
clothesline sway like elevator wire
and I feel more connected
by reading the stones that
shower a braille on my palms
as I tap the ground in withdrawal.

Good Riddance

I'm thankful for our encounter
and smooth seas
don't make good sailors,
you were a near
death experience
and nothing more,
you were always a story
that was written in sand on shore
and the tide that washed you away
also dusted off my spine.

Acrostic Depression

you wrote acrostic
poems in grade school
and thought it was pointless,
finding more than
one meaning in a
seamless word
whispers to you
and tells you that
it's not your fault
you were cheated on,
or why your
parents divorced,
sometimes instead
of 20/20,
a kaleidoscope
is the best way to
view yesterday's
circumstances.

Threesome With The Sun

I'm more or so
consumed by pleasure,
call me a hedonist but
my definition may differ
from yours,
contentment is subjective
and the objective
of attaining gratification
has dusted from belying
to sincerity and I've found
happiness in the way the
sun comes up
rather than the way
the moon can go down on you
and have you clenching
nocturnal bedsheets
with a beer
and a pen,

I take it all back,
no discrimination…
I'll be having threesomes with
the sun and the moon now,
give me my fix of both.

Sleeping With A Fan

she told me to write about
the happiest I've ever felt;
the happiest moment in my entire life,
and there is never such a circumstance
in its singularity that can be defined,
but in a string of circumstances
a definite divinity can be seen
through the cracks;
sobriety, the comfort of sobriety
makes me feel not quite as content
as the comfort of intoxication,
but the fact I can find refuge
in both is enough to make me,
the way the legs of my bedside table
are cut uneven and the way it
dances when I write,
the knuckle of my middle finger
kissing a hot coffee cup
in weariness, it makes me,
clichés and the cologne of
grass after rain,
petrichor and nasal-stained
memories make me,
a smoker's cough and phlegmy
clearings, mental crosswalks
with hands and I still walk
with my mouth,
that makes me,

the sky,
and the ground,
mailboxes with the flag down,
telephone poles with expired
promotion posters,
faux homelessness
in small towns,
leaves changing,
trees dying and
coming back to life,
how the wind feeds
conservation,
weeds growing in pavement,
dandelion stains on new jeans
or new jeans staining dandelions,
snowfall,
struggling to pick eggshells out of
yolk bowls,
pot and cigarettes
and they don't
go well together,
for me at least,
abandoned barns,
barns in use,
the sound of tires on
gravel driveways,
the strength
or lack thereof
to smoke when I'm sick,
it makes me,
the look of others when
I allow my dog to kiss my mouth,
the top fret of a guitar,

it's low and reminds me of
a child's cough,
wearing my fathers
stained white t-shirts
under 80 dollar plaid sweaters,
it makes me happy,
all of this and more make me happy,
but I still can't touch mirrors
and listen to the way I breathe before bed,
and that's why I sleep with a fan on,
for when you ask to turn it down.

Two People

my second personality,
he loves you
and I hate myself but
he loves you,
he told me the other day
where to find you and
I didn't want to look,
my eyes were burning,
but his throat was too,

I feel bad for him sometimes,
he doesn't think very clearly
but he knows how to write,
very well actually,
we have similarities,
we're liars,
our brains are the same,
kind of,
we wear the same clothes
for the most part,
he takes them off
easier though,
he likes to yell
and get angry
at nothing,
he hits things
and I wake up with the scars,
he's selfish, he doesn't

believe in karma,
he has no conscience,
he sits outside
and watches his breath solidify
and doesn't feel the weather,
he likes to bury memories
and then sleep with shovels,
I shower every day,
he doesn't,
I can feel him coming,
I have to go.

Cement Rose

I finally realized that
when I grip a rose,
the thorns are in my hands,
and the petals don't wither on their own,
I promise breathing soil and
give pale pavement,
few grow through the cracks
but don't survive too long,
some call it urbanizing,
but I prefer perpetual,
they feel heartbeats in the soil
and I've buried myself
in continuities,
and a stagnant earth
gives birth to a dormant death,
some call it wilting,
but I prefer realization,
no one compliments
the garbage in a
wind-coughed garden
but everyone steps over
a cement rose,
I'm still here
so the dirt is still beating
and I promise to keep
the trash off the sidewalk.

Ampersand

I respect therapists
like I respect anthropologists,
they dig and encounter an ampersand,
they can always inform beforehand
and foreshadow results,
but they found my bones
below 6 feet
and can't form an answer,
they knew where to search
they found the ticking finger
pointing at lazy fissures,
and buried blisters
but dripping shovels
keep raising a faded flag
that says:

"there's nothing here keep moving".

Circus Dance

ask a stranger if they've wanted to die,
and if they answer no, they're lying,
the inevitability of death has many
turning a blind eye to dying
or the thought of such circumstance
is a circus dance on a tightrope
with living ahead
and death below,
it has people trying to balance in place,
rather than walking forward,
and a visually manifested
tunnel vision view on life
is hard to come by
unless you've come to terms
that when you die
there's going to be a bit of happiness,
the tamed lions you know
are bound to turn on you,
and the trapeze is bound to fray
like the limbless man
who will eventually
wobble away,
and when
the only thing left
is a ring of fire and
the crowd is gone,
and falling off the rope is
almost inevitable.

A Man In A Trench Coat

a man in a trench coat
walked through construction
after dark,
dead branches grew
from the holes in the
end of his sleeves,
the night painted
over retinas
but his skin still seemed pale,
dyed dark hair
shined without hygiene,
and his boots
kicked debris,
I thought of columbine
when I saw his trench coat,
I saw guns and children hiding
I heard shotgun shells
breathing smoke
onto the pylons,
I saw brand new
blood-painted lane lines
in the middle of the road,
I couldn't make out his face
but I looked at a smiling maniacal,
and I was just driving by
and it seemed cold,
I had the window down for a smoke and
I smelled tired exhaust

from sleeping machines,
and it was then that I realized
he was most likely walking home
from work or going to get milk
from the convenient store,
perception will always drape over us
in a cloak, no one else can see,
it will never disappear and
to the trench coat man I apologize.

Weathered Skin

my moods change like seasons
and yet the weather stays the same,
it's the middle of summer
and my boots are covered in snow,
I'll wear toques at 30 degrees
and the chills don't
come from the breeze
but from kicking snow off
shoes on green grass
and realizing that nothing lasts,
it just always melts,
worrying about the
commonplace of tomorrow
makes yesterday the future,
so I never live in the past,
wearing a mask
so that the sun doesn't burn
my skin, it just sits and sets alight
whats has always been within,
the grass can grow under winter snow
but from what I know
there's no sun above,
so I ask myself why
I'm wearing this mask,
maybe the weather's never changing
and I'm just looking in the mirror,
I'm not wearing a mask,
I'm just growing a beard,

the snow never comes and
the green just disappears,
and what's left
beneath my feet is standing
on ceramic egg shells
slicing my toes is starring into hell
and the only way I'll stay
comforted with the weather
is standing still.

Dorm Room Cemeteries

adolescent women
below adulthood,
high in heels,
and validating
worth by regret
and planting
seeds in beds
of alcohol,
pulling over
sheets of hair
in dorm room cemeteries,
seeking acceptance
in snowless Januaries,
because the
beginning is
supposed to be
this cold.

Autobiography

I've quit smoking six times,
quit drinking four,
the intervals are
sparse and unworthy,
I wear jeans with
dainty holes
from cigarette butts,
my breath wreaks
of a mixture,
and my cologne
surmounts the
insurmountable,
I'll look skyward on
chilled nights
and try to decipher
between smoke and breath,
I'll purposefully wear worn socks
to give the sought useless
some worth,
I'll run soapy loofas
over scabbed knuckles
for punishment and end up
enjoying the sting,
I'll tie ties too tight
and my shoes too loose,
I'll scrutinize grammar,
and misspell because
hypocrisy makes me horny,

I pick at callouses until they bleed
I'll suck on bloody hangnails
cause I like the coppery taste,
I'll never litter,
and I fight at bars,
I drink alone now,
but I've quit four times,
allow me to put into perspective
that quitting anything
has moved from an elective
to becoming eclectic,
and new habits,
for me, don't replace
old ones but squeeze them in
to a car destined at a dead end,
but what doesn't kill me now,
makes death so much sweeter
in the finale.

Out Of Misery

I listened as a mouse struggled
to escape a half empty frozen coffee cup,
it took a while for me to understand
where the rustling was coming from,
I stared down the open lid
and saw glossy eyes
squinting up at me,
as if I was the sun,
and my first instinct was
to bring him outside,
I poured him on the frozen ground
and noticed as his legs were chilled, dead.
I placed him back in the cup,
put the lid on,
and exhaled,
giving him all the warmth
I could give,
his chest moving like
metronome trying to break
though his skin,
I could hear the ticking of his
heartbeat like a broken clock,
there was no chance,
his eyes opened and
stayed shut longer,
his legs stayed dead,
so I put the coffee cup
on the frozen grass,

closed my eyes
and stomped
like it was a cockroach,
I sparked a cigarette.

Frame

broken homes
are broken bones,
no christmas trees
and more ashtrays
than dinner plates,
handprints
tattooing arms,
hugging stair cases
over beer cases,
no shoe laces
and cut soles,
lingering souls
of what could have
been without neglect,
vines entwine her neck
and the kids tease her
for smelling like cigarettes
and her shirts are stained,
she sleeps on a mattress
only a mattress, no frame
of mind will remove
these memories
from the twenty-five-year-old
junkie you are now,
her parents OD'd when
she was thirteen,
her child has a beautiful name
and beautiful eyes,

and before mom dies,
I hope she gets
the right frame to sleep on.

Lines

I wonder what type of whiskey
the man painting road lines
at 3 am drinks,
am I stereotyping
or am I foreshadowing
my trip to the liquor store
in 10 years?

am I drawing lines
in the sand or pavement,
now?

our trips are the same.

The Man At The Publishing Company

what does the man behind his desk
at the publishing company deem
worthy of publishing and
how much are his shoes?
I wonder if my words
will entice him enough to begin smoking,
or quit smoking,
or have a drink,
maybe sign a contract
or rather have me one,
will he turn off his Bach
to understand or
turn up his Bach to understand?
will he analyze my grammar,
or the need of post secondary?
I wonder if he will bring forth
his obsession of
having a finger in his ass
to his wife after reading the erotics,
or will he put a finger in his ass,
will I be read in a
reader's digest in 25 years
while a man of elder
near shits his pants,
or will I be dwelled as an elder,
and I bet you they're over 200 bucks.

Calligraphy

pouring another glass
is peeling a hangnail
down with your teeth,
a monotonous suck
will only draw blood
to surface,
waking up is now
a common signature
on a death certificate,
a tedious magnificent
and I'm still here
and my calligraphy
is becoming spectacular.

Remembering Reefer

I remember the feeling
of reefer and sleep
or sobriety and insomnia,
it was one or the other,
a back deck stained
with eggshells and
whiskey candles
strapped to my tongue
and a flame burning
my throat,
eyes like lungs
inhaling a toke
and tearing with
black spit,
too fucking stupid
and fried to look at
a knife with malice
and then it was
only with butter
to smear on a sandwich
or uneven bread like
bong water in a glass for thirst,
in the microwave instead
of a toaster for some reason,
too fucking fried
too fucking dumb,
I felt better and quit,
no cracking eggs on deck tops

now it's beer can rings on desk tops,
like a marriage to dizziness,
I remember the feeling
of reefer and sleep
and paranoia,
depression
and anxiety,
and now a green smoke
is a double sided mirror
into the past of what
I used to feel,
and I'm spreading butter
on my conscience
and wrists
and neck now,
instead of being lifted,
I'm planted with dead roots,
no turning back
no speeding up.

Bar Hawk

she tears through
her insecurities
on fridays and saturdays,
shameless small talk
with bouncers,
and she dresses to fuck,
railing lines at pre drink,
and talking up free drinks
with horny hawks
circulating the scintillations
of spotlights for victims
of a cockcrow regret,
she picks and chooses
and it's easy for her,
finding a jawline
in a haystack seems
almost inevitable
when she did her makeup
in front of a mirror,
three hours prior,
she fills her empty
bed with cheap cologne
and sweat and gel,
only to empty again
three hours later.

Bar Past

I thought, "holy fuck man, look at yourself". The only change I ever witnessed for 3 years was the scrapings left ringing out on the bar rail. Always reaching out to a pocket for god and finding nothing. "I guess you can't refund the drinks, right?" She didn't laugh. I watched my circle get smaller, tired of the antics and my drinking became the butt of a joke. I watched my circle get smaller, my vision blurred like the future lining with a black vignette and with every drink I watched the bartender familiarize. Another? tap tap, an empty bottle uses its manners and mine, with a painted smile. Until close she would become my therapist, and the salary was almost the same for the two after I left. After close, the cooks offered sympathetic invites and lacklustre conversations at the strip club next door. They laughed and drank and like horny vultures, they watched their prey scale a poll like the fire they were fighting was inside. I saw no spark, no love given, no love received. I found it hard to love when hating myself was the only thing I loved to feel. The grease stained fries were tickling the back of my throat on the last night I went. I found myself puking next to a coke head doing key bumps and I asked through hiccups "does the smell back here not bother you?" he said "what smell?". I wiped my mouth and stumbled home somehow. I kicked broken pieces of pavement and scoffed at the curb-sides hugging garbage. I realized through the streetlights that my shadow wasn't the only darkness following me at night. Out of cigarettes and out of my mind I resented this city for having so many bridges. The screaming trucks below gave some sort of comfort with my feet tangling with the breeze. The stretching hands from out-of-place highway trees grabbed at me and I felt the world rotating. The night that changed me, a three am crosswalk flashed its hand at me, but I kept walking.

Growing Up

There was a time where I believed that friendship didn't flicker like a waterlogged outlet. Where standing up came before standing out. I never understood what growing up was for a long time. I remember when I was 15 and I saw a man at Starbucks spill coffee on his white dress shirt and thinking "fuck that I'm never growing up" and then when I was 18 I draped a plain white polo over my heart and watched everyone I thought cared about me redefine caffeine from waking me up to putting me to sleep. I insisted that success and money didn't go hand in hand and positivity is easy when the only thing you're paying for is young cigarettes and blindfold mints. When we grow on the outside, we shrink on the inside to a certain extent. We watch death like a shitty sequel. We fear the inevitable and watch the hands on the clock until they clap and your lights start to flicker. We swim in a bathtub of inconsistencies that drown our livelihood and when times become consistent, monotony sits in our throat like drying cement that cracks until we can't even breathe for ourselves anymore. Can anyone define happiness? And can you tell your kids that growing up is a breeze? Cause that gust of wind can blow the half empty cup of coffee on to your clothes and really fuck your day.

Common Darkness

like her childhood —
her future, she knew
would beat her down,
experiences forcing
her lovers to act
and practice lines
of rejection,
ignorance and companionship
coming together like
cutting out stitches too early,
trial and error became
all too common and
when she began to let
someone in, the house
was always too cold
for them to sleep,
the walls that
surrounded her heart
wasn't a wonder of her
world but a hell of theirs,
she couldn't blame the
footprints that would
always be viewed heel first,
and turn to herself for
being unable to let the past go,
one and then the other
the third and then
the forthcoming leaving

like november snow and
autumn leaves,
she felt hopeless
until her feet fit into
the shoes that were
were left behind by
a leaving lover,
she found a heart
that hurt,
one that lived in the
november snow
and dreamed about
orange and red,
she found shelter in
the homelessness of their
adolescent homes,
the shelter they shared
and moreover —
she realized that
the only light in her
life came from someone
suffering in the same
darkness she was in.

Why You Don't See Me Out Anymore

In high school and a few years after, I partied like it was '99. With a few friends and a lot of bad decisions. I found out how easy it was to provoke anger when the recipe called for a lot more than just a cup of whiskey. When I discovered what it was like to drink alone, I grabbed on to the opportunity like pulling nails out of a coffin, whether mine or someone else's. I glistened under scintillating hues watching horny bar stars get shut down like 2:30 am. I would laugh at the guys who would shit at the bar, I would watch fights outside like I had bets on them, until it was me. The entire experience was short lived and short loved. The hangover was never worth it, watching my bank account decline like my self-esteem when I realized no women there would want to talk about Karl Marx or Jean Paul Sartre's eyes on curb sides. I discovered that when looking at pros and cons, the flickering sign out front of the only bar in town fit the crime. I was tired of being tired at lunchtime the next day, I was tired of watching fishnets catch the first boner in the room, I was tired of eating shitty poutine and watching shitty fights prompted by shitty friends. Lonesome lullabies sang by fingertips fighting paper, waking up with the accomplishments of an empty mind instead of empty knuckles or empty hope. Out of sight, out of mind, I guess. The less I stare at that flickering sign, or flirting failures, sucker punches or bitch slaps, expletives and threats, six dollar rum and cokes, or bar boners and cum stained bathroom floors, the more I can focus on the party going on in my head.

Deceit

she's in those
pine floorboards
that cry to you
when your feet
whisper to the door,
she's in the backdoor hinges,
that weep when you
clench your jaw,
hoping she stays asleep,
she knows
and she loves you
and she's tired of being
stepped on and shut out,
disregarding warnings
from kin and companionship,
she's blinded by time like
is has room for deceit,
her skin tremors on
untainted bedsheets
'cause you're "working late",
she fills the empty spots
in her chest with
the swallowed tears
she hides
'cause she doesn't want to
show that she knows that
you're one-night-stands
are about as meaningful

as the kisses you give her
when she pretends to be asleep,
be weary,
you have nothing without her
your friends will fade
your moments will
fade with the light
flickering above your ego,
and soon you'll
find yourself dragging
cinderblocks on pine needles
and leaving through
the front door.

Similar Sickness

sadness like cancer
or an infection,
catch it early and
you'll be okay,
let it linger and
you'll find yourself
drawing conclusions
on chalkboards
with fingernails,
and writing farewells
on eyelids and trying
not to blink.

Callow & Murderous (II)

As a nosey mother fucker, I find myself observing more than I should. Over analyzing like a hypochondriac at a screening for cancer. I sit and watch as wardrobes are chosen by standards and literacy is on its deathbed. Clouds of perfume follow 12-year-olds, $800 phones and paying attention to the inattentive as if it had a dollar value. Compassion is falling through the cracks from heavy feet, dragging like credit cards over glass tables. More interested in mind altering than altering mind, we have become the bane of progression. Fixated on fixing what isn't broken and breaking what's perfectly fine. Watching lips and ass grow with each episode or issue. Watching ribs poke through the adolescent girls like the needles they're foreshadowing. Vomiting up lunches still made by their mothers and blood isn't even flowing yet. This world is backward, experience is a guide for love as if it doesn't differ from body to body, depression is hip, death is glorified, sadness is weakness and breaking hearts gets high-fives. There's always a diamond in the rough but it's cutting the glass and we can't stand our reflections anymore.

Fathoming The Fall

you can only
fathom the
meaning of love
by comparing it
to the moment you
fell apart.

Fearing Death

I don't fear dying but I fear watching everyone around me leave. I'm tired of watching the hands of time bound this throat of mine and you can only see through an hourglass if the sand's at the bottom, and the grass on other side isn't greener. Through death is a heavy heart, how contradicting where empty can bear weight. My skin is stretching like stone, my eyes are dragging cinderblocks with footsteps, and my blinks are becoming longer. I can't fathom a life without death, it's been part of us since the beginning but grasping the concept is like holding onto a blanket of fog for warmth. The thing about death is that though they flow backward in time without stepping forward, their voice follows you every time you watch their photo like a blind man watching a silent film. Every time you listen to a song, see the sun peek through clouds, hurt, and pain adopts everyone. I'm tired of hearing their voices in my head, in my heart, and not conversing. You can only talk to the absent so long before you go insane.

The Broken Ones

The worst part about pain is feeling it in others. Watching their eyes sink like pennies in a fountain, and wishing that the promises for a brighter future given by the grinned ones weren't empty. With misery comes sympathy and digging yourself deeper comes as a result of digging others out of their hole. The hurting want not the shared shattering of hope to become a hairline in anyone else. We sit and watch this fracture in our conscience slowly inch towards a break and walking over glass makes rock bottom seem like fucking memory foam. We can see it, the broken ones, we share something, we watch each other and say nothing, we look young and feel brittle and we know we want death to greet us like a zealous acquaintance we've watched dance for years. When you pull to a red light and see scarred knuckles on the man beside you, and you make eye contact, you watch the dirty man with dirty bags drag his will on the steaming sidewalk and you almost grin. You pass the business man pulling his child like a dog and understand where he'll end up. We all hurt, we dress differently, and handle it like adults. We're young enough for a target on our backs but old enough to expect the gash. When life fucked us, they left in the morning leaving only the smell of cigarette, and a note. "thanks for everything"

Success & Jealousy
_____

I'm getting to a certain point where the path
traveled has a spherical momentum. A carousel of
bullshit and bills. Each day mirrored to the next and
yesterday is just the violent stepbrother. Bullied by
the consistent cries for change and I was never the
one to give in to peer pressure. A tangible outlook
on an altered future brightens itself with every
moment of companionship sitting on a blurred line
of opposite success. Watching others succeed like an
old man living too long and seeing death in
offspring. A sight like staring through the stained
glass on a church and begging for forgiveness. I've
always lacked confidence but I know I could have
done great things. A malevolent relative puts a fist
through vices and bullying always came from a
rough past. Around we go, getting dizzy from
regularity and even yesterday had a yesterday. I
can't stop pacing, my mind is racing and it seems as
if the finish line stays in sight but I'm running
backward.

Sleeping Sentient

I thought about thinking one night while trying to sleep on a bed made out of pins and needles. Sinking through the quicksand of the memories embedded in the sheets. It was dark out when I laid down, and the sun is peeking through the horizon now. Sleep is a diamond in the rough and the needle in the haystack is weaving threads through yesterday and sewing them to the resentment of today. Watching the clock dictate a proper time to disregard the sweat and have my eyes shut out the visions of who I could have been. I hear the birds singing a symphony of lullabies and they're failing. It's not their fault, the sun is their mother and my maudlin midwife, giving birth to the shred of fatigue baring unconsciousness until noon. A bed frame made of wind chimes, tossing and turning a striding scream into the spineless faux that give it a purpose. A victim of midnight, and a casualty to the callous night that I familiarize the martyr of my memories with. The medication of a shittier day constitutes a shittier night and it's wearing off and it's time to sleep. I swear the sheets were dry when I died and I'm reborn midday. Prompting bags beneath pernicious eyes. "Rough night?" "Yup".

Broke

I stared at my empty wallet with bitter irony, full of
receipts and useless collective cards. Save money but
spend money! Declined stamped in red across the
debit screen hitting like domestic roadkill and a lie
spirals through consistency about calling my bank
this morning "they said it should be fine!". Like a
nineteen-year-old in a black dress carrying high
heels back to her dorm, I swear those doors took an
hour to slide open. A mourning to a dead account, I
sit in my car with my last cigarette stamped to my
lips because I can't fight with my chest in public.
Transferring twenty dollars from my savings and
"damn, the bank works fast!". I can reload on
cigarettes again, pay day is tomorrow, I thought.
Stressing over the hydro bill seems only pointless
when even with the lights on I live in darkness.
When we die our money dies with us, the memory is
of who you are, and how you lived. I may be broke,
I may not drink your expensive gin, but I can live
with who I am and never think what could have
been.

Complexity In The Toughest Of Times

complexity conjures
us all into giving up,
we all ignore the
glistening whispers
that tell us everything
is fine — where perplexity
portions the tough times
into moments that
hit the hardest,
blinding the whispers
and turning them
to the screams
we listen to,
dragging us to the depths
of adversity with no strength
to climb.

<u>Cold Deceit</u>

a cold cerulean rain
falls from deceit,
filling every crevice
in your body with
the fear that stops
you from ever wanting
to get your feet wet again.

Dawn

I break until
the break
of dawn
and when
the sun rises,
so do my walls.

My Biggest Fear

my biggest fear
is having you view
me as I view myself,
staring at a mirror
to shattered vision.

I loath familiarity
and I fear consistency.

Empty Chest

in a shell, you'll hear waves
crashing together in a
hedonistic symphony
called a current,
all pulling you to a
different current,
listening to this
wind chime soliloquy
that dances with
every stride through
the vast blue can get
you through storms,
grey clouds have no barring
to the white-headed curls
that wash away every dark
thought in your head,
press your head against
my chest and you'll hear
emptiness like hearing a
noun isn't a rarity, you'll hear
a fading beat, one that shaves
itself with time,
press your ear against my chest
and I bet it's not the ocean you hear
my thoughts and my hopes will echo
like a whale's cry, unheard by billions.

The Great War

the battle between
mind and heart is
a war that can ripple
in the affect of where
you might end up,
there's a different type
of repetition in the
crime committed
by commitment
and you're always
framed and you're
always the victim,
live like your
mind never robbed
your heart from certainty,
like your thoughts never
held your eyes hostage
to stay staring low,
live like the bloodshed
in battle showered
your conscience with
lessons and lesions
will stay closed as
long as your mind
is open to change.

I Am Negative, I Am Positive (Sea Sick II)

a broken vessel
and bailing water is drowning
out the ability to drift back to shore,
it's always calm before the storm
but when a breeze disappears
the chance of moving anywhere
flies away like the seagulls
laughing in cocksure,
the water seems so thick
like drifting in ink that draws out
abstracts of stagnancies
and every time I row,
the boat rhymes in harmony
with the singing current
and cisterns will begin to cry,
I can't travel alone and
I don't know how to swim
and positivity in a broken heart
is preferring drawing over falling
because sand is softer than
rock bottom.

Toxicity

breathe in
the toxic air
like you wished
your lungs had ears,
and listen to every
scream you swallowed.

Broken Homes

too many childhoods
with just houses
instead of homes,
finding their heart in harm
and if you're skipping stones
with broken bones,
sleeping through
silence or screaming
hurts the same.

Peace In Pain

I found peace in pain
and hope in suffering,
it made the end seem
easier to reach,
until I realized
that the light at the end
was only a reflection
of the past paving a
way for the future.

Free Falling

forever suspended
in thick air and
altitude has no bearing
on breath because
I'm never held high,
a masterpiece at
my own malevolence,
cutting heart strings and
falling in unison,
stretching skin with
hair waving like
grabbing the attention
of the happiness lost
for so long,
living in air can
only condition
your chest for so much,
slipping into,
from thick to thin
the longer the fall
the harder the hit
and how can it
be called free-falling
when in love it
costs so much.

Stormy Heart

she's spinning
like a top on
a silk sheet,
wrapping everything
around her in
the storm that
brews with every
beat of her heart.

The Ghosts Of The Next Morning

little ghosts
cutting holes
in bedsheets
to scare
and prepare
for when
the bedsheets
cut holes in you
when you grow up.

S(cent)

It doesn't matter
how rich you are
when you fall in love,
the worth comes
from the value
they hold you to
believing in yourself,
the faith in entirety
can cost you your life,
when looking and
planning for your ever
the robbery of what
you were saving
can send your stock
plummeting to worthlessness,
an empty pocket doesn't
hurt as much as an empty chest
and throwing change into
a fountain only seems fitting
because I though I never would
but if I had a penny
to my name
it would be your scent
that brought
me to richness again.

Going Down With The Sun

find yourself
someone who likes
when you forget to
shave your legs
because it tickles
their cheeks when
the sun goes down,
find someone who
fucks your demons
and you,
find the tailor that
sews your sweat
to the bedsheets
you're holding on
to like a bad memory,
find that the bad memories
float to nihility in the
air being split by
orgasms,
find that when the sun
goes down on you,
and the moon goes
under the sheets and
that your past lies
under the clothes
on the floor.
Drunk Tattoo

anxiety is wet sand seeping
through a growing hole
in a sieve of positivity,
anxiety is a rotting
cutting board jammed
in your throat,
where every breath
chopped into pieces
decays in the pit
of your stomach,
lasting like migrating birds
arriving to find snowfall,
a rape victim of hands bound
by unmet expectations
and spines realigning
to throats and throats
plugged with damp cement
and every time I speak
it dries a little bit more,
the english language is
written by children
and broken branches
carving into the back
of my throat with
no way out,
I've never viewed my
ribcage as prison bars
until now,
I've never been
locked out by my own walls

until now,
and this sickness is breeding
vines all over any guard
I try to knock down, it's not
contagious but it will wrap around
your heart like a drunk tattoo.

<u>Why</u>

I get asked a lot
why I started writing
and the answer is simple,
instead of my arms,
the pen bleeds,
and instead of myself
I hang words on
dotted lines that
sway back and forth
in stanza.

Roadkill

I read people
like I read roadkill,
with compassion first,
and then with thoughts of
how stupid they must
have been to end up
where they are now,

then again,
I guess they
were crushed by
something they
didn't think would
crush them.

Weeping Willow

she helped him
grow like a willow
while she wept
and watched him
sway his oxygen
into someone else.

Fenestella

her legs
wear tattoos
of backseat
stitching as
drainage hair
paints faces,
searching
for love in
automobiles
parked behind
churches
or grocery stores
and only finding
comfort in
fogged windows
that give
no reflection.

Confidence In A Cavalier

this world will
get so much bigger,
just find the front
seat of his car
and look out the
window.

Unedited

an unedited
version of her
was thrown at him,
he lined the margins
of her thighs with
criticism and dotted
the i's with his tongue;
her moans crossed his t's.

Mood Rings

she had mood rings
in her eyes and
different hues are
different cues to
her subconscious
to run from anything
that shows her love.

To The Hard Taught Young

Little boys confusing ignorance with masculinity. In a world where boredom breaks hearts, you'll be left with regret when you're left alone. Trust me, kids, I've been where you are and suffered for years because of it. It'll really start to hit you when you hear the rumours, when you show up to a first date and end up staying and drinking alone because their best friend reminded them of the reputation you have. Fuck and leave, fuck and leave, fuck and leave, it'll become noisome when the only smell that reminds you of love is the cum breath screaming back at you because you asked if she needs help finding her keys and she doesn't even have her bra on yet. Listen to me when I say this, your friends that give advice like a priest telling the naive about marriage, they don't give a fuck about you, they're just so bored with their own life that the stories of stinging the conscience of girls barely old enough to own a credit card will give them the confidence to proceed with being the dick head that they are. Your heart will slowly fade, it will slowly descend into the pit of your stomach, into the pit of where your emotions are hiding. You'll eat microwaved dinners without change, your eyes will see a reflection and regret and it will fuck you and stay. Something different, huh? Watch as you keep breaking hearts. Watch your life will begin to slowly mean nothing to anyone desiring love, and eventually, you'll desire love.

The Lack In Others

there's flaw in
the architect
that assembles
insecurity in others,
not in their work
and those who
feel the need to
shed their skin
are usually the
one's bit by
the snake.

The Sacrifice For Beauty

no lover leaves
a rose garden
without blood
on their hands.

Immune To Ignorance, But Surrounded

growing amongst,
like blowing between
dead dandelions,
glowing amongst,
like staining a
blade of grass
yellowhaired,
and what shines
is your laughter,
I hear the glitter
from your tongue
scrape your teeth
around the dull,
your cheeks
and your lips —
and goldcrowned!
the sky becomes
a shade lighter
with you around,
and the past, too

you're a rose pushing
through a drought
holding wholesome
while watching
others dig holes,
some too deep to
hold their heads high

some too deep
to let any light in.

Find Hope

find hope like the child you were,
and rest in the mind of a youthful bloom,
stare up your half empty cup,
and let in what will fill the vacant spaces
from a parched past.

find hope like you had before the bills
before the debt
before the 9-5's
before drinks on tuesdays
and the tears on your baby photos.

find hope like it's an x on a map
and look for it in your own heart,
you'll find it in others but it'll leave,
look for it in rain
look for it in asphalt drawings
that chalk the past with a gust of wind,
look for it in rolling tides
and in your eyes.

find it and run,
run away from the past,
run away from advice
run away from pointless sex
and shitty music
and shitty friends
because with hope,

you need nothing else.

Drunk On Deceit

he furnished her
with spilled lies;
just enough to
fill her to half empty —
intoxicated with deceit
sleeping on landmines
and living in a body with
skin too tight,
searching for comfort
asleep on stone
alone with no shoulder
to call home anymore,
she's too full
and every lover
from thereon
will sit on a
blurred line
and she'll
stagger away.

Brains Of Sand

I put my brains
in grains of sand and
maybe that's why I get
the look I do when I tell
people of the past
plans for the future,
with age, shadows
become reflections
and the rejection of
tomorrow becomes
the darkness that
follows behind me,
I put my brains
in grains of sand
and I keep turning
them over for a measurement
of the time I have left
or rather the time I've wasted.

Down By The Water

down by a lake
in July with a cigarette
I remember eating through
a bottle of beer
or rather, a bottle of beer
eating through me,
like a boat zip-tied.
to a dock, insecure is
an understatement,
and with waves curling
like slugs and tablespoons,
coming undone is
almost inevitable,
pine needles showered
under shoeless feet
and I listen to a domestic
between bullfrogs,
drunk cries from
across the island
echoes through out
this stillness of the sky
the water
and my mind,
a moment to dwell
and think
in isolation, it can be dangerous
to leave me alone with my thoughts
but when I'm sitting with the stars

and the beer
and the laughing
winks from lighthouses
it only seems that peace
can throw itself through
my veins like skipping stones
and I only sit on dewed docks
with moonlight
because her relationship
with the water is much more
kind to my reflection then
the sunlight is.

Questions Of Regret Or Reverence

I hate hating myself
and I love pain,
is it vain to hate
who you are,
but love how much
you're suffering

does anyone
really even understand
what it's like
to be happy,
or do they
just comprehend
the ability to
be less sad? —
and will death
be the mediator
between the two?

and when we're
lying six feet under
will it be with
regret or reverence.

Hometown Suicides

when I was seventeen I went to
the hospital at 3 am,
I only had my license for a year,
I should have been driving
to the harbour,
smoking cigarettes
with a young love,
not myself insane,
I opened my chest up
to traditionalism that
told me my thoughts
were out of a movie
or from "hormones"
"you'll grow out of this sadness", he smiled.
and a visionary of feet dangling
like wind chimes crying for help,
he said it was just a breeze,
I'm a grown man now,
sitting,
drinking a beer,
smoking a cigarette,
listening to shitty
sad music at 2 am
with a gut full of gusts
blowing these chimes,
singing me to sleep
thirteen miles away from
a doctor that could have

saved me from years of pain,

how many hometown suicides
have I read about,
could you have saved?

Good Mourning

sleep is a destination
only traveled to
through sanity
and the ability
to stomach the
sight of what you see
without seeing
anything at all.

If Touch Could Lie

if touch could lie
and pain could
lie next to you
would you be
sleeping in a
bed of glass
or beneath grass
and tears?
whose name made
you drink to forget yours?
whose touch drove you
away from touch, entirely?
who planted your seed
under a doormat,
in front of a door
that you keep knocking on? —
you know who it is,
and you keep knocking.

I Want Peace

I want the wind to blow
like she's never coughed before,
I want the sky to cry
like she has no reason to,
I want the ground
to breathe and grow
like a planter and
a windowsill,
I want the ocean to
dance with the currents
pulling seas and bays
together like seems that frayed,
no plastic frames
depicting throats,
no famine in water
like dying bulbs,
no crochet blankets
to keep the light out,
just dreams,
because we're floating,
just dreams because
it's all we have.

Don't Get Lost

I'm the rough you
have to travel through
to get to the diamond —
and they haystack
hiding the needle needed
to patch your wounds,
don't prick your finger —
don't get lost.

Then & Now On

he traces her scars
like they were stars
in daylight —
like she heard
the moon tell
the clouds to disappear

he then planted a rose in the
pit of her stomach and it
didn't bloom until he left,
jamming the thorns into the judgment
that coated her eyes.
and she took the interest staring back
thereon — like a pill,
hoping to overdose,
but only waking up with
a churning of nauseous regret.

<u>Broken Lungs</u>

I live
and breathe
regret like
my lungs are
coated in
broken promises.

Laughing Stocks

I bought shares
into the laughing stocks
when the muscles
in my face taught me
to smile,
time decreased worth
and evolution put happiness
in a jaw made of glass,
wired shut,
the eyes in my throat
stare to the grass on
the other side and
it is in fact greener.

<u>Carousel</u>

wilted and watered
wishing for more
wishes upon wasting,
falling in love
to be lifted up and
then tied down,
a breath after cigarettes
and a hangover,
I live standing on
a carousel without power
and I still get dizzy,
a mentality made from
oxymorons and
a life can only
be worth living
if you're willing to die.

Graduation

if you look
back on time,
time won't look
back at you,
treat yesterday as
a high school friend
that graduated from
friendship as well,
care not about what
cares not about you,
and treat tomorrow
as a new start from
the mistakes you
left in a bottle or in
a broken heart.

Dying Art

I was told
that poetry
is a dying art,
so consider me
a deadman
with a pen
and only a fortnight
of clear wrists and
a closed neck

dear,
ignorance,
the work
is alive and well
but it's the worker
that dies a little bit
word-by-word.

A Smoker & Blood

every time I see her
it's like a smoker
and a bloody cough,
red-tipped curled napkins
laying the foundation of
what to say
or what to do

why was I left for dead
and why did I survive?
why will I never be
good enough?
mobile and coherent,
but the stench
of a rotting mind
is helping me
heave

maybe it's not
the cigarettes,
maybe it's the
throat slit heart strings
telling me to tuck the
past into the hole
I was left in.

Present Decisions On Past Mistakes

don't
   claim
to know
me well
or to
        love me
when you
haven't
    seen
    me drunk.

Cum & Go

little boy,
dreaming of sex,
dreaming of more sex,
and of blowjobs,
condemning love
with your parents'
liquor at a party
before midnight.

you will regret
your restless zipper,
when it replaces
your heart in half
and see, finally,
how easy it is
for someone to
cum and go.

A Run For My Money

It's 3 am and I'm sitting in my garage and the smell
of wood bleeding is overcoming the fingertips of my
nostrils. I'm reaching out towards anything that
gives me life. I'm smelling and sniffling and
coughing through the phlegm of sickness and over-
smoking. Instead of walking 20 feet and pissing in a
toilet I whipped it out and drained my body into a
coffee cup I found under the lid of a garbage can.
I'm watching a bottle of Jack at my feet flex through
club lights and I may go home with it. My night has
broken no consistencies, I'd say difference would
give me a run for my money but I don't run and I
don't have much money, so variance will stay tucked
in between the ashes on the ground and between
the wet coughs that blow the cigarette smoke
around like ribbons at the talent show daddy
couldn't make. My thoughts spark with lighter fluid
this late, and I'll drink my whiskey without ice cause
the ice machine makes too much noise and I don't
want to wake anyone up. I'll keep running these
thoughts through the prairies of rotting wood, ashy
cement and garage doors that play the victim of
domestic knuckles and the anger that flows, holding
hands with the whiskey. I'll wrap my mind around
how picture perfect this night is for a poet but I
don't really consider myself a writer, just a unstable
motherfucker who writes poems, I'm just a human,
just a man trying to release the dancing demons in

my mind that somehow sway to the harmony of
hurt.

The Truth Hurts

I've been called
crazy
a sociopath
psychotic
insane
worthless
dead
emotionless
and demented

and as a man,
it upset me

and as a poet
I was thankful.

The Devil Fucks Hard

sometimes I feel as if the devil
lives in my skin,
goosebumps are needles,
and I'll put a bullet in his head
if it means I can sleep,
I stare at strangers and
I'll feel tremors above my bones,
slitting throats
and bullet holes
and chicken wire being
eaten by throat skin,
nails painting pictures on pavement,
alleyway morgues and
buying new shirts,
stained hands
and a ton of soap and water,
ever-sleeping bodies rotting
in my nostrils,
finding peace
from secondary 6 feet,
the devil lives in my brain,
whispers and pleas and demands
and screams,
the devil lives in my hands and
ties nooses of my own hair around
my own fingers,
the tearing serenades and I'll never pull fast,
so it's a long song that pains me to sleep,

the devil lives in my eyes,
seeing sounds and
screams turn my head towards,
pupils grow
and grow
and grow,
the devil is fucking me, hard,
so dry, yet oceans in december
flow under my skin in the summer,
he's pulling my hair,
leaving scars in my skin,
leaving me sane enough
to realize the thoughts are wrong,
the devil is fucking me and I'm a hedonist
and my dick is soft,
the world around me is black and white,
and when the devil lives under skin,
in my brain
and my eyes
and my hands,
he paints the horizon red.

Medusa In Lust

memories like
anacondas
and hair that
wraps to your fingertips
to numb the need
to touch and
turn to stone,
a simple graze
can lay the foundation
to a rocky bottom,
and her eyes wander like
baby hair in the wind,
an iris fire can start
from a little spark
to parental affection
like a lifetime of
legs like dead wood shutters
and the wind,
her cries for help
hide in chimes and a
tiny gust can disguise
lust as love.

The Nine To Five Jive

work to live
and live to work
off the hangover
on a nine to five,
barely overhang
expectations to
someone who feeds
off the explanations
of a nine thirty arrival,
dance in a bedside ballroom,
of denial about the morrow,
live in sorrow
and pity yourself,
get lost in the
lipstick stains from
the bottom of a beer bottle
on your nightstand and
you cant stand night
but the sun shines twilight
on priors redefining colours
darker than black.

Coke Heads

they're both
addicted to coke
and their fingertips
are nostrils,
feeding off the addiction
of peeling back the skin
that drapes their hearts
like spring jackets
and snow,
selfish lovers,
trying to steal
shields of organs
that don't fit in the end,
their hearts are exposed,
and relationships hereafter
are bedsheets
over windshields,
thereon.

Love Is A Rope

love is a rope
and it pulls you
closer to death,
and you cant let go,
it burns your palms
and you can tie
her hands down with it
as she screams
vibrations into her thighs
and her eyes roll back,
it can sit above dangling feet
and it can tighten your shoes
and help you run,
love is a rope,
the only rope that
frays without use.

love is versatile.

Hide-N-Seek

the demons in
my head and
everyone I know
started a game of
hide-n-seek at the
first thought of suicide
when I was 13,
and every piece I write
is a paper trail
of hints to point
you toward where
I'm hiding.

Flood

she shot me
in the heart
and expected blood,
but she was living
in a flood of her own
too deep to notice.

A Wedding Or Funeral By The Water

love isn't anything
more than a flower
at a wedding or
at a funeral and
a broken heart
is a broken vessel
who keeps bailing
out the water,
even if they're
filled with love.

Foundation

strength isn't
accompanied by
a past of beautiful scenery
and oceans
and clear skin
without scars,
a building must burn
before you can find
your foundation
for the next
in the ashes.

Desperation & Weakness

desperation and weakness
go hand in hand like
unknown palms
and party bedrooms,
like razorblade solutions
and bathroom tiles,
unmade beds and a stench
that stains your fingertips
and your eyelashes
and churns your stomach
to vomit up the morning breath
of the night before.

Strange Addiction

I have a strange
addiction to sadness,
I knit quilts of
the past and circumstances
and wrap myself with it
before bed to stay cold.

Waste Of Space

your presence
in my past is
a waste of space,
like talking astronomy
with a mechanic
as if orion's belt
made my
wheels turn.

Immolation

she was
the pilot to
a paper plane
when you
could still
smoke inside.

The Night We Died

the stars got high one night,
and told us we were dying,
they stared down and saw us fading,
they looked to each other and
talked about that the harder
we are to see, the closer we are to dying
and I was almost transparent in their eyes,
supernovas come commonplace
and the night we exploded,
I'm sure many others did too,
the grass was breathing
and never inhaled,
I screamed and
the stars went dull,
she screamed too,
I saw constellations through
the veins in her neck
and put pictures to her words,
and she just quit smoking
and I sparked a cigarette,
we spoke about dying
but we were already dead.

A Way In

she made me view
bridges and buildings
as infrastructure instead
of a way out,
she had a rabbit
running around
it's hole instead of
practicing how to tie a noose,
she put a 24 hour sun
in a continuous winter solstice,
a mind used to darkness
received a glimpse of light
and I've never spoken highly
about a sunburn until now.

Two Flies & A Cricket

two flies are fucking
and the colourless tin
full of cigarette butts
replaces my nose,
elfin thoughts and
no liquor,
shadows of dancing curtains
arouse paranoia
and a quarrelsome cricket
tries to fly,
stars sit and scream
sights of clarity,
and I'm clapping at a mosquito,
the only time an applaud
accompanies failure,
tactful antics of a
lonely mind
can only watch
two flies getting off
before jealousy
begins to kick in.

Organ Donor

she's an organ donor
without a spine
and he tore pieces
of her heart out,
gave it to another
and ran away,
he came back
and missed her,
he found an empty painting
and nothing was the same,
the pictures on his walls
are always changing,
collecting hearts
of past lovers
and he's blind to see
that his own frame
is becoming vacant.

Wishful Thinking

the headlights
on cars are
shooting stars,
and on
saturday nights
I take drives
because I hate
drunk drivers
and myself.

Hollow Rain

the bruises sit
in a hollow rain,
slowly floating
from my throat
to my spine,
standing weakly
with no mouth
to straighten
my back.

Banana Bread

love
is not logical,
like a toque
and summertime,
or picking a rotting fruit,
but sometimes it
gets cold at night
and bruised bananas
make amazing
banana bread.

Trust Is Like Fire

people change
like seasons —
and trust is like fire
you can warm your
hands on it —
or it can burn you alive.

Assisted Murder

I constantly sit
as a mass murderer
in a maze of mirrors
with only a pen and urges,
and if you look at who
I have let into my mind
you can see that I support
assisted suicide.

Born & Raised

I was
born and raised
a rat
at the bottom
of a birdcage,
I grew up
staring at
feathers falling
like snow,
watching others
fall and fly
and wondered why
I kept crawling
and reaching for
an open ceiling.

Valentine's Day (Alone & Together)

(I)

being alone
is much more
than being on
your own,
it's a vacancy
sign hanging
on your heart
waiting for a
curious driver
to stop in
and unpack
their mind
and stay forever

(II)

cherish the feeling
of flowers and
the evening ,
the puzzle
fit of palms
and thumbs
fiddling,
find beauty
in losing direction
in their eyes

and tracing
their veins
like road maps
to a destination
of finding beauty
in a mirror.

A Sixty Nine With The Sun

when I fall asleep,
the morning
comes faster
than a sixteen
year old boy,
the days go by
like trying anal
for the first time,
and when the
sun goes down
on you,
it's like having
a one night stand
at your own funeral.

A Letter

this is a letter
to my future self,
start digging a hole
or just send me help,
you won't notice me,
I'm not the person
you see in the picture
with mom and dad anymore,
the smiles aren't real,
I'm a lot taller and
I haven't grown much.

Morning Sickness

I discovered
morning sickness
at one o'clock
in the afternoon,
I sleep with myself
every night and I thought
it was just a one night stand
when I was sixteen,
but he fell in love
and curls up like a
snail in sunlight
before bed.

Waves

her sadness
came in waves
and she saw
the ocean
in his eyes

some days
she would
drown and
some days
she would
swim

some days
he would
hold her
head under
and some days
he would
leave.

The Suicidal Nihilist

a suicidal
nihilist
fell in love,
they were
a match made
in heaven,
and it really
made me
question the
credibility of
infinity when
I cut myself
open and counted
the rings.

I've aged terribly.

<u>"Pain Makes You Stronger"</u>

anyone who
has told you that
pain makes you stronger
hasn't clutched
pillows and bedsheets
with skin dripping
from fingertips,
they haven't had
crooked thoughts stitch their
spine to mattresses,
they haven't locked
every momentary shred
of happiness behind ribcages
so they can come back
and then leave the key
in the hearts of past lovers,
they haven't clutched on to
vices like it was the grip
of yesterday that kept
tightening them to death,

pain has made
me gain weight,
walking on a tightrope
of twine for years,
the frayed ends are
tickling my feet and
I'm not laughing,

life is just a waiting game
until it snaps or you fall,

fuck off, it doesn't.

Inspire Me

inspire me,
wrap your lips
around the head
of my pen,
spit ink,

gag on metaphors,
bring me to life again,
dig your nails into
my back pages,

let me lick your
fingers as you turn pages
with subtitles like foreplay,

read in between my lines
and trace the scars on my spine,

let me write
about how you look
when you're curling
your finger at me
because you're not finished
reading yet

and scream when you
you're fucked so deep
in thought that the words

vibrate off the page
and slide down
your stomach.

Thinking Of Death

she was one of the first
to stick around when
she found out my past,
when she found out
who I was behind
the tattoos and the long hair,
it shocked me,
I shocked myself,

sometimes we have
to watch our entire life
fall apart before we
can rebuild it again,
and the ones who laid
the foundation
tore it from beneath us
like a tablecloth and
broken glass,

why I am no longer
thinking of death and
why is death no longer
thinking of me?

Who I Am

I smoke a lot
I drink a lot,
and fuck you
if you have a
problem with it,

I own too much plaid,
I smell like
overpriced cologne
and cigarettes,

I have long hair,
patchy facial hair,
and calloused hands,

sunday mornings
bring crusty chest
hair from dried whiskey
and most of my socks
have holes in them,

I used to be this person
because I was dead inside,
I'm breathing now
and habits become lifestyles,
and fuck you if you have a problem with it.

Car Accident

our relationship
was a terrible
car accident,
it had the police
calling my mother,
it left scars on my body,
and no one expected
me to survive,
I was driving
for too long and
fell asleep behind the wheel,
you walked away
without a scratch,
but I walked away
with wisdom,
I drive carefully now,
and I have a passenger
I'm willing to drive
a lifetime for.

Acquired Taste

I'm a learn to love
type of person,
a red wine and
sleeping pill
type of person

I'm a hard one to love,
I'm an acquired taste,
I'm angry but appreciative,
I struggle to pay bills
but always pay attention.

the first is hard to look past,
but I'm not all too bad,
and what you need
I'm not all, too bad.

I will love with all I can,
I'll take the road
less traveled to your heart,
and it's a rocky journey
but a coffee and cigarette will
turn night into day and
I'll be there through it all.

North Dakota Pipeline Crisis

dead in spirit,
now dead in flesh,
nothing can regress
landmark and emptiness,
feeding families water
through the siphoned
throat of greed,
dripping down beaks,
a black devil standing on green
and force vomiting mother earth,
heaving up any
sign of life and faith
and motive,
dead feathers sinking to the mud
in graves of slime,
dead feathers on heads,
dead feathers are targets,
stunted childhood
born in blood,
born in oil,
stillborn after birth,
death for convenience.

http://standingrock.org

Contributions to the standing rock sioux tribe can
be made here:

http://standwithstandingrock.net/donate.

<u>Breathe</u>

lungs in.

fucked like
she's hated
and fixed
like she's
loved,
her eyes
mirror no
longer bathroom
tile but blink
at sweat dripping
from his brow,
she has found love.

lungs out.

Spin The Bottle With Dreams

I played
spin the
empty bottle
with death
and ended
up kissing
the devil
inside my
skin.

you know,
I used to
have company
in the dark,
myself and
shut eyes
and dreams,
it's hard to
anymore when
everything
you used to
dream about
is now a
nightmare.

Cold

if you find the rain
in winter
and see grass
grow through
polluted snow,
you will finally
understand
what it's like
to feel cold
in a body with
blood boiling
at 98.6 degrees.

Bars & Cocaine

I had booze
bars,
cocaine
and sex
take some
of my friends,
I miss a lot of you
but fuck you for leaving,
you defined perpetual
pain in seeking
friendship
in fiction,
and it made
me into someone
stronger and
surrounded
me with better people
so thank you, too.

Clouds & Vacation

I don't think ahead
'cause I've been
left behind,
I have no names
for my kids yet
'cause I'm a cloudy
day and a vacation
look up just to be
disappointed,
I'm rain on a beach
leave your footprint
and then go home.

Clear Criminal

I'm a criminal
with a clear record,
only stealing
opportunity from
myself like
the death penalty
and a chocolate bar,
a nine to five probation
for attempted murder,
and I'm still breathing,
I'm an apostasy
for a religion where
god is success
and I'm still sitting
on burning aspirations.

This Room

this room we sit in
is covered in trees
and cars
and mothers,
roads
and babies,
casinos
and bars,

it has eyes,
the walls can't
hear your cries for help

it can see
your suffering
wallets and
your tears at
your grandfathers funeral,

this room isn't forgiving,
it survives on your pain
and your blood
and lack of sleep,

the walls are caving in
and the floor is becoming hot.

The Subconscious Foreshadowing

I was fifteen when I had
   my first drink,
like a serial killer
   with dad in the backyard
firing guns at
    crying trees,
or carving pumpkins with
mom in the kitchen

I had
no idea.

Homeless Gambling

you were nothing
but a homeless man
and a gambling addiction
and your chest is
your wallet,
your heart is made of
copper and doesn't
mean much to
anyone anymore,
you threw your past
in your back pocket
and your future
pays the price.

Sad Song

for days like today,
days where the skies cry,
and you find mirrors
in dark clouds,
days where you
feel nails scraping
your ribs like chalkboards,
reaching from your heart,
days where mornings
are yesterday because
you refuse to wake up,
turn on a sad song,
feel the weight sinking
in your chest,
feel your stomach
churn and dance
with every chance you
had to be a better person.

What I Wish For You

I have a friend,
he bruises her brain
and fits her for
gloves and razorblades,
he fucks her and
his advice is
leaving for work
early in the morning,
his steak doesn't bleed enough
at dinner time
and she's a cunt
and eats backhands
and bleeds enough
for the two of them,
she holds back tears
for makeup while
he masturbates
and they're engaged,
he went fishing with
a net when he was eighteen
and only caught her.

Don't Be Too Quick To Judge

they laugh over
candlelit dinners,
he wears salt and
pepper coats
and black jeans,
she doesn't wear
makeup often
and her glasses
are too big,
she reads
and writes
and high school
called her a virgin,
a prude,
she's been with him
for seven years now,
he chokes her and
she sucks on his fingers
after he searched for
a light switch in the dark
on the inside,
his back leaks
like she does afterward,
he leaves handprint tattoos
on her face and spine
and spits in her mouth,
she sat in the back of
the class quiet,

away from the bullshit,
every day with thoughts
of how she'll set the
fuse on his cock that night,

don't be too quick to judge.

Heart Valves & Beehives

anxiety is your chest
and the heart valves
of beehives,
and the honey that
hardens in your throat
as you're stung
every time
you take a breath

the bees that
hold your tongue hostage
will wither and die when
stinging,
it's just a matter of time
before the hollow bodies
of short breaths
will fall to your stomach
and you can finally
breathe again.

The End

everything is okay
in the end and the end
is inevitable,
life is a blurred line between
a double sided mirror
and an interrogation room,
and you're cuffed in front of yourself,
the scars are stars
shining light on
memories that lead you into
the twenty-seven breaths you will
take while reading this,
you are not alone,
the distance from
skin to bone is
easily traveled,
and a roadmap of veins
will carry you to
the light at the beginning
of the tunnel, pick up your phone,
call whoever,
receiving a phone call
at 3 am is better than
a wet phone in the morning,

you are never a bother.

Writing With Razorblades

she can put pants on
over the scars on her thighs
and wear long sleeves in
the summertime,
but to hide the scars in her mind,
she has to scribble a smile
and hang weights from
her shoulder blades,
she chats with burdens
at midnight,
and she was never
the talkative type,
she wrote in a
leather-bound notebook
under tough skin,
she met the devil
and he said it wasn't
good enough,
so she kept writing.

The Aura Of A New Start

you gave tangibility
to ambiance
and build an
atmosphere around
my conscience
with only
your breath
and a heartbeat.

Daddy Issues

she's tired of
hearing "daddy issues",
she met a man,
it was take your kid
to work day
and she stayed
home and watched something
that was being worked on,
he left,
and her parent teacher
interviews in grade school
was a turned table of
questions to a
single mother

home is where the heart is
but no one's ever home,
she doesn't miss him,
she met satan
under her will
at a party
first year of college,
she doesn't want
to walk herself
down the wrong path,
she left,
she met a man,
and doesn't want to

walk herself down
the isle and
she doesn't miss him.

Twenty Years Later

he got chlamydia
from a whore on
the road and
drove with it
in his dirty truck,
the eighteen wheels
spun the infection
into his ring finger,
he rewrote his vows
on prescription paper
and they got cured,
and diagnosed,
the disease spread
to their nine-year-old
who doesn't believe
in love anymore
because santa has
to go to two houses,
with two moms,
with two dads,
and in the back
of a truck in
twenty years.

Ugly Is A Desk At Night

I'm ugly
and my habits are ugly
my teeth are cigarettes
and I smoke white
and breathe cardio,
I'm ugly
my voice is an earthquake
and my body is third world,
I have nothing
I am nothing,
my existence is
fragile,
my chest is a dinner plate,
and I keep finding
hair in my food,
sexual fantasies
are rarities,
I dream of
killing people
and saving animals,
my thoughts revolt
and revoke constantly
and consistently,
I live in a monotonous
monotone hymn
spoken by a pastor
in my mind
and organized religion

is a fucking farce,
your bible was written
by third world
muddy fingers and
my body is scarred
in verses that mutter
tedious manners,
hold the door for me
and I'll say thank you,
I'll slam it in your face
and I'll make you
thank me.

Raining Feathers

I met myself,
I was thirteen, I tried to meet god,
of course, that's when I believed,
I shook hands with myself,
in greeting, I found out
the secrets that have
yet to be buried,
I just tried burying myself

I walked everywhere
with nice shoes and
muddy footprints
and heaven wouldn't
stand for it

I got to know myself better
over the years,
we became friends
for a bit and drifted
apart and below,
we reunited again

I was sixteen,
I turned my knuckles
and arms into colouring books
and I had no problem staying
in between the lines;
I drew them,

The Corner Of The Room

I said sorry
I accepted and
we moved on as friends

seventeen,
my dad hung a body sized mirror
in my room,
seventeen,
my dad hung a coffin
in my room

I was eighteen and I dug
six foot holes into the
drywall and buried
the empty coffin,
we all have that friend
we don't see for a while,
we cut contact like
a feather in the wind,
but the wind stops
and an acquaintance
fills the dead wing
with ink and comes
looking for me again.

Hijacker

I've been called insane,
I've been going down
in planes hijacked
by past relationships
and how my wings
were clipped by
expectations,
I flew too low
and ended up
destroying everything,
I sit in a burning vessel
making love to the ground
and torching any hand
that tries to help me.

Hypocrite

I say
"the past is the past"
yet I'll put bullets
of scenarios
in a gun of tomorrow
and put it in my mouth
to deep throat,
hypocrisy teases
the trigger
and I have a
stomach full
of regret,
I'm gagging on yesterday
and I'm killing myself
with jealousy.

Ceremony

I can't tell if
it's the insecurities
or if I'm a blind man
drawing pictures with a
dark crayon on a blackboard,
the moment I meet someone
who remotely connects with me,
love is a poor tattoo
that slowly fades over time,
and I feel that only my linework
is erasing itself from your mind,
we met in retail
and love at first sight to me
was god up until then and
I'm a faithless man,
a daily progression made
death a procession that hit a wall,
your voice gave the
night's hopeless a place
to rest his head,
at a time where I fell
in love with hating myself,
your touch gave population
to this empty city
and authenticity to a
fake complexion staring
back at me,
if a time ever comes

where your eyes
tell your heart that
she was wrong
or where your bones
flow with blood
at the thought of me,
I'll know I was your validation
to look me in the mind
and tell me that I was right,
I want the sight of me
to sit on a pedestal
so you can stand it,
like college
I seem exciting
until you begin
working at me,
a majority drop out,
but some stay,
don't leave,
please graduate with me,
this ceremony wants
hats thrown up,
not dirt thrown down.

Drink

drink for life
drink for death
drink for wanting to die
drink for waking up hungover
and wanting to die,
drink to sickness
drink to health
drink for yourself
drink for pain
drink for suffering
drink for the posters on you
walls and their wandering eyes,
drink for tomorrow
drink for yesterday
drink tomorrow because
you didn't drink yesterday,
drink for falling in love
drink for a broken heart
drink for breaking hearts
drink for her
drink for him
drink for mom
drink for dad
drink because you miss
and drink because you're not
just fucking drink.

Change & Regret

she found
love in bedsheets
and found regret
when the sun rises,
yesterday she said
she would change
and she did
just that, tomorrow,
in front of a bed
that wasn't hers,
looking at the past
like a dead fly on
a windowsill,
if she looks forward
she can see a sun shining
but she's so fixated
on the hollow body of prior
that desire sits within it.

Snake Skin Past

I buried the past
and called it a new start,
subconsciously throwing
dirt over my shoulder
prevents the future
from blooming,
a snake in the grass
slithering through my mind,
sheds its skin
and leaves remnants of
a past life scattered
above the surface of soil
and the stench of death
is starting to become
unbearable.

Pendulum

a pendulum is stuck
swinging between
a rock and a hard place
and my eyes are fixed
on the ticks that
mirror your voice,
the consecutive grazes
on each wall;
your touch and
I'm looking into a mirror
without cracks and
knuckles untouched,
I'm beginning to
see you within myself,
you're buried under
layers of skin,
swimming in the blood
that refuses to break through
the surface like before when
the pendulum stood still.

Wet Pavement

I'm ugly on the
inside
and feel ugly on the
       outside most days,

the thoughts
drip
down
from my mind
to my throat
and harden
like cement,
a barrier of
regret to punish me
for every time
I let my tongue
push a cry for help
through my teeth
like wet pavement,
don't let it harden
in your brain,
just leave your
handprint like a
innocent child
trying to leave a memory.

Weathered By The Weather

lonely autumn
and rock bottom
and the leaves
never change
unless the
weather does,
blowing skin
from breathing
trees and seeing
the rain fill an
already brimful chest
can pour forth
emptiness faster
than being drained.

Lost & Found

I lost my wallet
last sunday and
I lost my mind,
I lost my virginity
when I was fourteen
and I lost my pride,
I watched a homeless man
shit his pants last summer
and I lost my appetite,
I watched a man
stain his wife's face with
his problems and
I lost hope,
I lost my friend
to a shotgun
and my aunt to cancer
and I lost faith,
I lost a battle to
a bottle of pills and
I found regret
in the morning,
I lost my sight when
I watched a man
put a gun in his throat
and lose his skull,
I thought I lost the world
until you found me
and I discovered my everything.

<u>Don't</u>

if you ever sit stagnant
on the question of whether
or not they're

"the one"

don't.

you'll know when
anxiety is carried away
through gut walls
with the wind of
a butterfly and her wings

you'll know when you
look into a mirror of hue
and see the healing scars
in your eyes cure
colour blindness

you'll know when radios
are reminders and
your skin dances with the
dimples they hate

you will know,
you will feel

every organ come together,
you will feel your lungs
stitch to your fingertips
as you trace their body,
you'll find portraits
in abstract paintings
and you'll no longer
see abstracts
in your
portrait.

How Does She Love Me

I smoke cigarettes and they
say that one cuts your life eleven
minutes short,
I light them with barbecue lighters,
I wear toques and shorts
and have very straight teeth
but they're slightly stained,
I drink and yell and hit things,
I throw teddy bears at sunshades
and fuck drywall 'till it cums,
I have a planters wart
on the bottom of my right foot,
I read books and hate religion,
I eat hotdogs on slices of bread
and say that I need to change
and never do,
I drink pepsi at 10 am and
whiskey at 11,
and find negatives in positives,
I have facial hair patched
like a quilt and phlegmy coughs,
I appear hard to love at first glance
and at second glance I'm still
hard to love,
I sit to pee 'cause im lazy,
I hate bars
and love pubs,
I hate drinking

and love drinking,
and I'm indecisive,
I've quit smoking six times now,
I masturbate too much
and have cigarette burns
on the ceiling of my car
'cause my aim is terrible
and I cum on her leg sometimes,
I eat the green of watermelons
and swallow apple seeds,
but she fixes the cracks
in my hourglass,
she makes mirrors
and morning breath bearable,
and waking up to her
is adding eleven minutes
to my life.

How does she love me?

<u>Drug Addict</u>

if you weren't a
drug addict before,
you are now,
and instead
of through
your nose,
they'll enter through
your heart
and you won't
look back
until it's too late,

you will relapse
and it will fuck you
up the same.

A Mirage Greeting

sleep evades me
even when morning
cums too quick,
another sip or
dip into something
that takes me
away momentarily,
take me away
I ask before falling asleep,
every fucking night,
good intentions are
fatigued at misinterpretations,
I'm an empty book
with a hell of a prologue,
a vacant hotel
with bright stars
and stained carpets
and bedbugs
and no shower curtains

I don't want the
facade or mirage anymore,
one that people
wave their hands through
in disbelief,
I want you to understand
that every cigarette
is a cry for help,

every thank you
is an apology
at liquor stores,
and that my foot
gets heavier
when a set of lights
are close to cumming.

Real

broken homes are broken bones,
no christmas trees and more ashtrays
than dinner plates,
handprints tattooing arms,
hugging staircases
over beer cases,
no shoe laces and cut soles,
lingering souls of what could
have been without neglect,
vines entwine her neck
and the kids tease her
for smelling like cigarettes,
her shirts are stained,
she sleeps on a mattress,
only a mattress, no frame
of mind will remove these memories
from the twenty five year old
junkie you are now,
her mother overdosed when
she was thirteen,
her child has a beautiful name
and beautiful eyes
and no father,
and before mom dies,
I hope she gets the right frame to sleep on.

Relapse

I've blamed others for my sadness
and I've blamed circumstances
for my drinking,
when I only have myself left to blame
I slip into a glass that's half full
of denial or
half empty,
I search for pessimism
and sit content with sadness,
I get phone calls at 2 am
and drink beer at 3,
the hardwood floor
hugs me and holds me closer
than anyone ever has,
it's a strange addiction
that I can't seem to shake,
the only thing that will
overturn feeling a frozen glass
with velvet fingertips
is feeling her linen thighs tickle
like hummingbirds between mine,
I eat up this strange
comfort of being alone
and she's the only thing
that feels like a relapse.

Wet Eraser

I live in
constant concussion
under the head
of a wet eraser,
the past always
leaves a mark,
no matter how hard
you try and forget.

Old Woman

an old woman
with grey hair
and ashen eyes
is churning my stomach
like a cauldron of thick bile,
sucking my skin through
my ribs inward like a zit,
she's running feathers
over my flesh,
turning pours
into potholes
holding every tear,
pushing goosebumps
like vines and sidewalk cracks,
she carves bags
under my eyes
like dating a gravestone,
she stopped breathing
for a while but
let a sigh out
on the back of my neck
and I puked up the past.

Floating

she puts me on a pedestal
and makes five foot two a lot shorter,
I don't deserve the world
but I find myself orbiting regret,
I can't continue to
beautify alcohol
and cigarettes in my writing
but beyond the white page
is something black,
I look back on every
yesterday with the willingness
to be able to relive
or not live at all,
I'm indecisive and petty,
she says I don't need to change
but the clothes on my back
are dirty and worn,
instead of taking
my shirt off,
she stares into
the fabric tears
and sees something beautiful.

I don't understand,
I never will,
I stand still and
feel as if she has
a rope around her hopes

and she's beginning to sweat,
I don't deserve the world,
she said I'm hers,
I had a bar set
and she sits above,
floating,
I'm indecisive and petty,
but I know I need
her in my atmosphere.

The Street Light That Never Changes

I go out for
a cigarette
and there's
an intersection
that I can see from
my back deck
every night,
the facing set
never turns green
unless there's a
car waiting
and it's like
looking into
a mirror.

Momentary Monologue

every morning she performs
a momentary monologue
in front of a mirror
to a tough crowd,
she sings a soliloquy
to the same crowd
every evening,
tremors and oil
scrape her skin,
she unpins hair
and sits in front of
a tough crowd,
the sought to satisfy
lays awake on the moon
and sleeps on the sun.

Senseless

there's a blind man
living in my head,
he makes my decisions
for me,
there's a deaf man
living in my heart
filtering every "I love you"
into a lie,
the touch of a senseless
man can bring
about senseless
feelings towards a
defenceless guard,
turning sight into
breathing and
taking deep breaths,
and what you once
thought was a horizon
and a path to painlessness,
turned out to be nothing
but an eyesore staring back,
the heart hears
what the heart
wants to hear,
and though
he can read lips,
he cant break the sight
of the truth rotting behind teeth,

what an imagination my senses have,
fictitious fairytales plot every character
as an antagonist and the the man
in my head cant even see the play.

Raking In The Wind

she placed
freedom
within the veins
of the leaves
she tried to
rake together
in the wind,
but her feather
hid within the breeze,
building bridges
where there
should have
been walls.

Hot Headed

oh the fucking
doctors that
have tried to force
me to get help,
anger management;
like taming a lion is
better than leaving
him in the wild,
surrounded by
provocation is
as if I'm a walking
defence for a
clear murder
and there's blood
on my hands,
vile thoughts
constitute vile
words and
tangible is far
from emotional
but a hole in drywall
cries out like a rape
in an empty hallway,
echoing death is
foreshadowing a
dark future like
treating the holes
in the wall as

a looking glass
into who you
are and who you've become,
I blame it on passion
on love
on rye
on others
on religion
on three lined poems
on him
on her
on fucking
on breathing,
to bring about
philosophical answers to
simple-minded questions,
and for fuck sakes
I'm only hot headed
because the hell
in my mind
is burning brighter than
the heaven in my heart.

Beg For Me

I just want to be
the one begged for,
for once,
I want to feel the wind
hit my spine,
instead of my chest,
and in the clarity
of the sky I just
want nothing,
instead of watching
a drifting cloud
come out of the woodwork
and pour rain on already
damp skin,
I want the paragraphs
at 2 am,
I want to listen to
pleas
and cries,
I want love to chase me
for once
and I want hatred
to run,
I've been
surrounded
by clear knees for
as long as I
can remember,

I want to set
myself on fire
and see flames in
your hands
instead of
your eyes.

To Alex

forever in our thoughts
like a lingering idea
never acted on,
loved by all and
too young to take
another path,
a moment leaving
but forever sinking
deeper and deeper
into bone and vein
without experiencing
the smile or the laugh
that painted an original
on anyone lucky enough
to witness,
18 years with much more,
a future staring back
like love at first sight,
each hairpin freckle
will sparkle our thoughts
with memory too bold to forget,
a life too cherished to let go,
never to be forgotten,
etched into forever like
an echoing whisper
in an empty hallway,
your absence is a pain
beyond tangible,

an instance
beyond nightmare,
like a little sister to me
a best friend to many
a daughter
a sister
a cousin
a niece
to nothing but something only
capable of love,
forever in our hearts,
always in our thoughts.

To Alex, Friends, Family
and every heart holding
her smile forever.

12781089R00208

Printed in Great Britain
by Amazon